# GRIZZLY BEARS

# GRIZZLY
# BEARS

*An Illustrated Field Guide*

JOHN A. MURRAY

ROBERTS RINEHART PUBLISHERS

Copyright © 1995 by John A. Murray

Published in the United States of America by
Roberts Rinehart Publishers
5455 Spine Road, Mezzanine West
Boulder, Colorado 80301

Published in the U.K. and Ireland by
Roberts Rinehart Publishers
Trinity House, Charleston Road
Dublin 6, Ireland

ISBN 1-57098-029-2
Library of Congress Catalog Card Number 95-67336

Distributed in the United States and Canada by
Publishers Group West

**Library of Congress Cataloging in Publication Data**

Murray, John A., 1954–
Grizzly bears : an illustrated field guide / John A. Murray.
p. cm.
Includes index.
ISBN: 1-57098-029-2
1. Grizzly bear.   I. Title.
QL737.C27M87   1995        599.74′446
QBI95-20069

To the men and women of the Park Services
of Canada and the United States
whose job it is to protect the kingdom of the grizzly.

## Books by John A. Murray

The Indian Peaks Wilderness

Wildlife in Peril: The Endangered Mammals of Colorado

The Gila Wilderness

The Last Grizzly, and Other Southwestern Bear Stories
(with David Brown)

The South San Juan Wilderness

A Republic of Rivers: Three Centuries of Nature Writing
from Alaska and the Yukon

The Islands and the Sea: Five Centuries of Nature
Writing from the Caribbean

Nature's New Voices

The Great Bear: Contemporary Writings on the Grizzly

Wild Africa: Three Centuries of Nature Writing from
Africa

Out Among the Wolves: Contemporary Writings on the
Wolf

Wild Hunters: Predators in Peril (with Monte Hummel
and Sherri Pettigrew)

A Thousand Leagues of Blue: The Sierra Club Book of
the Pacific

American Nature Writing: 1994

The Sierra Club Nature Writing Handbook

American Nature Writing: 1995

Grizzly Bears: An Illustrated Field Guide

# *Table of Contents*

As a nation, we have emphasized and extolled the abstract qualities of wildness—space, solitude, wildness, diversity, beauty, and the aesthetic and spiritual bonds between man and primal nature. These values are essential to man's well-being, and perhaps ultimately to his survival. But also imperative is a better understanding of the biological complexities and natural order governing undisturbed nature. Only through a holistic comprehension of the complexity, diversity and oneness of wilderness can we hope to preserve it in perpetuity from the consuming forces of a resource-exploitive society. Moreover, by understanding the ecology of wilderness we can better understand our habitable environment with its man-wrought changes and thereby aspire to a dynamic and imperishable habitat for man and for other forms of life.

—John J. Craighead, *A Definitive System for Analysis of Grizzly Bear Habitat and Other Wilderness Resources*

# Preface

WHATEVER I KNOW OF GRIZZLIES HAS BEEN learned primarily through observation. Books taught me the names of plants. Museums preserved bones and hides. Researchers explained how a complex organism sustains itself in a challenging environment. All that was important. The most valuable experience, however, was acquired by watching bears in the field. Personal observation, as Aristotle believed, is the most reliable source of truth. It was not unusual for my field observations to contradict what I had read or been told, especially with respect to bear behavior. For the most part, though, the empirical bear was consistent with the scientific or literary bear. I have sat on the cold spring ground and photographed a sow grizzly as she nibbled horsetail sprouts from earth that ten days earlier had snow on it (see photo on page xxx). Her cubs were all around and I palpably felt the warmth of the maternal bond. I have watched in amazement as a boar grizzly dragged the remains of a spike bull moose across a meadow and into a forest. The only hold he had on the carcass was a bit of neck muscle in the teeth. I have videotaped a young female grizzly as she successfully battled a subarctic wolf for possession of a caribou carcass. I have watched grizzlies play, fight, eat, sleep, nurse cubs, explore, make love and go about their daily affairs in the wild, and I am deeply appreciative. Each sighting has been a gift, every moment a privilege. I never tire of watching grizzlies, or of sharing them with my guests— other naturalists such as Rick Bass of Troy, Montana, David Rains Wallace of Berkeley, California, and David Brown of Phoenix, Arizona.

This book is designed for the lay person, as a guide book to generally introduce you to the world of the grizzly bear and coastal brown bear. Like any guide, it is meant to be carried in your pack, or kept conveniently on your car dashboard as you drive through grizzly country. It is a book meant to be used. It represents the natural culmination of a lifetime of studying and watching grizzlies. After five books on or relating to the species, this is probably the last I will do. It is my final opportunity to share with you, a fellow lover of bears, some of my photographs and thoughts on grizzlies. In that sense it is a very personal work. The chapters are arranged much as brief modules in an introductory course—the university professor in me—and each contains a thematic collection of photographs. The appendix provides a bibliography that is worth exploring, should you have further interest in specific aspects of grizzly bear ecology. Some of the finest naturalists in North America have devoted their lives and writings to this species. There is no substitute, however, for viewing bears firsthand, even if you have no other place than your local zoological park. I would also recommend a visit to grizzly country. Sometimes national forests can provide a better environment for learning about grizzlies, insofar as they attract fewer people than national and provincial parks. Even if you don't see any bears in the wild, you will normally find ample evidence of their presence and activities, as indicated here in the sign and food chapters. Discovering and evaluating this data can greatly enhance your understanding of the bear and the world it inhabits.

During the six years I lived in Alaska I accumulated over 300 hours of observation time with grizzlies. This included trips to the arctic coastal plain, Gates of the Arctic National Park, Arctic National Wildlife Refuge, Kenai National Wildlife Refuge, Kenai Fjords National Park, Chena State Park, and the Alaska Range. By far, most of the observation time occurred in the Alaska Range, where grizzlies are visible along the 90-mile road that bisects the northern range of Denali National Park. This invaluable experience would not have been possible without the assistance of managers in Denali National Park and Preserve. I would like to thank the following officials: Ralph Tingey, George Wagner, Bill McDonald, Tom Griffith, Russ Berry, Ken Kehrer, and Ralph Cunningham. Fred Dean, a former colleague at the University of Alaska, Fairbanks, generously shared his extensive knowledge of Alaska Range grizzlies with me, and always provided up-to-date reports on bear activity. Rick McIntyre, who for 14 years was the chief ranger/naturalist for the west end of Denali, became one of my closest friends. He and I often photographed wildlife on his days off. I'll never forget our days together on Stony Hill and Thorofare Pass, following Big Stoney and her cubs. Whether we were huddled around our tripods in the midst of a sleet storm or idly swatting mosquitoes on a sunny day, Rick was always a true gentleman and the perfect bon vivant. Two other friends in Denali made my time more enjoyable: cinematographer Bob Landis of Billings Montana, who has the eyes of a hawk and the energy of a hummingbird, and photographer Michio Hoshino of Tokyo, Japan, whose conversations and marvelous photographs taught me new ways of looking at the grizzly. In Colorado I must thank biologist Tom Beck, who proofread the grizzly bear chapter for my 1987 book, *Wildlife in Peril: The Endangered Mammals of Colorado*, and who shaped the words into something worthy of their subject. In so doing he led me to become a better natural history writer and more rigorous thinker. A special thanks to Paul Schullery and David Peterson who read and commented on the manuscript. Finally, much appreciation to my family—parents and son—for their love and support over the years.

(Note: unless otherwise indicated, all photographs are by John A. Murray.)

# 1

# AN IMMENSITY
# OF MUSCLE

## *Grizzly Bear Physical Appearance*

The bear was about a hundred steps away, in the blueberries, grazing. The head was down, the hump high. The immensity of muscle seemed to vibrate slowly—to expand and contract, with the grazing. Not berries but whole bushes were going into the bear.

—John McPhee, *Coming Into the Country*

IT WAS A BLUSTERY LATE AUGUST DAY. I WAS HIking in the Alaska Range near the head of Igloo Creek. The sky was overcast. There was the smell of snow on the wind. The tundra was flushed in Oriental tapestry colors—the bright orange of dwarf birch, the salmon red of crowberry, the soft yellow of alpine willow. I had spent the morning picking blueberries on the north slopes of Cathedral Mountain and had crossed Igloo Creek, intending to explore the backside of Sable Mountain. I was new to the country and was roaming wherever curiosity took me. There was a little side creek that drained the heights of Sable, and so I followed it into the highlands. I hadn't gone far when a band of Dall sheep came running over a charcoal-colored ridge further up the valley. Just as I was pulling the binoculars out of the pack something lumbered over the ridge behind them, paused for a moment, and then proceeded down the slope. The Dall sheep raced by me, headed toward Cathedral Mountain. I brought the binoculars up. It was a grizzly! My first in Alaska. The hump stood out prominently. On the open tundra the extended claws were clearly visible. The shaggy coat was sunbleached nearly blond. Behind her came two cubs, colored identically to their mother. They were only slightly smaller than the matriarch. For the next two hours, I was in John Murray's version of heaven—alone on a mountainside with a good pair of binoculars and a trio of berry-eating grizzlies within safe viewing distance.

To see a wild bear is always exciting. No other animal so powerfully evokes the North American wilderness. For many people, whether in Yellowstone, Banff or Denali, the sighting is so brief—a burly shape crossing a ridgetop glade, a dark form angling through an avalanche chute, a bulky animal standing in the forest shadows—that positive species identification is elusive. You may have seen a bear, but whether it was a black or a grizzly, a male or a female, a mature or a subadult animal, is difficult to determine. Naturally you want to at least have some certainty as to the species. Whatever other information you can acquire as to gender and age is also valuable. Here are some helpful suggestions that may help you evaluate and classify your bear sighting:

- In the field, one of the most striking aspects of the grizzly bear is the pronounced shoulder hump. Be cognizant of the fact that posturing can cause a black bear to appear to have a hump. Consider this in analyzing the feature on the bear you are observing. The shoulder hump, by the way, is caused by the muscle mass on the upper back which gives the grizzly its important digging and dragging power.
- Another distinguishing characteristic is the sheen of the coat, which is caused by the silver-tipped guard hairs. As the grizzly moves over the landscape, the coat can appear to ripple and shimmer, even on a cloudy day. This can produce a flashing, semaphore effect visible at great distance.

- Grizzly bear foreclaws are sometimes bone-colored and sometimes more darkly stained. Because of their unusual length they often can be spotted when the animal is walking on open terrain or engaged in feeding or exploratory activity. Black bears have shorter, recurved foreclaws which are not as distinctive as the extended foreclaws of the grizzly. Grizzly bears have the ability to grasp objects in their foreclaws much as if the claws were fingers. This becomes noticeable when the bears are feeding on blueberries or soapberries, and reach through the branches to pick a particularly large berry.
- Grizzly bears have a concave facial profile, as contrasted with the convex facial profile of the black bear. The grizzly forehead rises at an oblique angle from the base of the muzzle and creates a break in the line of the face, causing the "dished" effect. In some cases, however, large black bears can appear to have a concave facial profile, so this method of identification is not always as reliable as some of the others.
- Color is not a certain indicator as to species. Grizzlies come in all colors, from white to brown to black, and everything in between. Some adults have frosted stripes on the opposing front quarters. Others carry portions of the "ring collar" (a colored ring, usually white, around the neck) into adulthood. Grizzlies can also have a multi-colored coat, with various patterns over the body and legs. Similarly, black bears can become sunbleached and cinnamon-phased black bears can present a grizzly-like appearance.
- Carry a camera when hiking for the purposes of accurately classifying grizzlies. I recommend at least a 200 mm telephoto lens (and a tripod) for use in the field. I normally use 50 ASA Fujichrome Velvia or 100 ASA Fujichrome. Kodachrome 64 is also good. The telephoto lens should be as fine as you can afford. At first I used an inexpensive 70–300 zoom lens, but with mixed results. A 300 mm f2.8 produced much better images. Videocameras with their powerful lenses and low-light abilities, are also ex-

Black Bear. Note the coloration, with the jet black hair (cinnamon is another common variation) and white heart fur patch. Also note the massive and somewhat dished head shape, which would complicate classification based on head shape alone. With cinnamon-phased black bears, a common color variation, mis-sightings are not uncommon.

Adult male grizzly. Note the black hair color variation and the foreclaws.

The blond hair color variation in a subadult (3 year old) grizzly bear. Note dished face, evident even in the subadult facial profile.

The light brown hair color variation in an adult female grizzly bear. Note the hump, which is sometimes visible at great distances, and the concave facial profile.

The dark brown hair color variation in an adult female grizzly bear.

The reddish brown hair color variation in an adult female grizzly bear.

Grizzly cubs early in their second summer (June). At this point the cubs weigh around 70 pounds. Note: all bears in this sequence are from Denali National Park. Elsewhere average weights may be more or less.

Grizzly cub in its third summer (July). At this point the cub weighs from 150 to 200 pounds.

Adult grizzly in early autumn (mid-August). This is a female accompanied by cubs. Notice the size of the head with respect to the rest of body. Compare this with the same ratio in the previous picture. She will weigh over 350 pounds by denning time.

cellent devices for identifying grizzlies. Also, many naturalists carry spotting scopes, in addition to binoculars, to more closely observe bears.

- Almost all of the adult grizzly bears I observed over six years in Alaska weighed between 300 to 500 pounds. I know this because researchers generously shared their field data with me. Like many mammals, grizzlies exhibit sexual dimorphism (weight differences by gender), with the males tending toward greater size than the females. The difference in body size is most evident when grizzlies are observed mating (see photo). Males appear about twice the size of females. Grizzlies that weigh over 700 pounds have been documented, but most continental bears are less than that. One day, Denali National Park ranger Rick McIntyre and I were photographing a 225-pound, foiur-year-old female grizzly on Stoney Pass. A tour bus stopped beside us and one of the passengers exclaimed, "Look at the old boar grizz! He must weigh 700 pounds!" The man actually believed the subadult female was a mature male. It has been the unfortunate fate of the grizzly to have everything about its nature wildly exaggerated. Try not to add to the confusion. If you photograph a bear, especially one with a radio collar, query the bear biologist for the park or forest. Chances are, from the photograph, he or she can give you an exact body weight. It may surprise you.
- Gender identification is possible visually. While body size is only a vague indicator, there are more accurate methods. I credit the following tip to my former colleague Dr. Fred Dean, emeritus professor of wildlife biology at the University of Alaska, Fairbanks. If you watch a bear for a long enough time you will see it eventually urinate. This is your opportunity to make a judgment as to the gender of the animal. The urine stream of a female jets backward away from the posterior of the bear. She will also posture her four feet closely together so that she appears to be standing on a small pad. In this way she will not wet the thick hair in that region of the body. Males, on the other hand, urinate forward

and under the stomach. They extend their four legs outward, arching the body in a bridge-like fashion so as not to wet themselves. In both cases, the animals assume a rigid position while relieving themselves.

- Gender identification based on head shape is also possible, but more difficult. Males have a more robust skull than females, and as a result their heads have a blockier, more massive aspect than females. The females have a smoother, more contoured head than the males. Acquiring the ability to differentiate gender on this basis can take several seasons in the field, and there is considerably more room for error than with the previous method.

- Another indicator of age is the roach, a flap of long hair hanging from the throat. A mature animal may have a roach, although not all adult grizzlies develop this unusual feature so often portrayed in paintings.

If it is inconvenient for you to visit grizzly country, you can still observe grizzly appearance in two other ways. The first alternative is to visit your local zoological park. Because grizzlies are relatively easy to maintain in captivity, they are among the most popular attractions at such facilities. Here you can photograph, sketch, or simply watch the animals as long as you wish. Watch how the bears move, how they look at things, how they interact with each other. Such a visit is good preparation for a trip into grizzly country, and can prepare you for understanding the activities you observe in the wild. Not only can you study the grizzlies closely, but you can also compare and contrast their appearance with that of the black bears, which are normally held in adjacent areas. The second option is to tour a natural history museum. Again, these are present in most major cities. The grizzly bear habitat group, or diorama, will give you a dramatic sense of grizzly appearance, and also of the grizzly's home environment. There is no substitute, though, for the real thing. See the appendix for a comprehensive list of areas in the United States and Canada where you can observe grizzly bears, or coastal brown bears, in the wild.

# 2

# WHEN THE COUNTRY COMES ALIVE

## *Grizzly Bear Sign*

I recall the first bear track I ever saw. It was my initial day afield in McKinley Park and my brother and I were crossing from Jenny Creek over a rise to Savage River, on our way to the head of the river. One lone track in a patch of mud is all we saw. But the track was a symbol, and more poetic than seeing the bear himself—a delicate and profound approach to the spirit of the Alaska Wilderness. A bear track at any time may create a stronger emotion than the old bear himself, for the imagination is brought into play. You examine the landscape sharply, expecting a bear on every slope as your quickened interest becomes eager and enterprising. The bear is somewhere, and may be anywhere. The country has come alive with a new, rich quality.

—Adolph Murie, *A Naturalist in Alaska*

GRIZZLY BEARS LEAVE EVIDENCE OF THEIR PRESence on the landscape. Even if you never see a grizzly in the wild, you can still learn to interpret the signs of their passage and note the scope of their activities. Indeed, this is one of the most important lessons to learn with respect to the natural history of the bear. An educated observer who has not seen the resident bears but who has studied the empirical evidence can often speak more intelligently about the local population than someone who has seen bears in the same area, but who lacks the knowledge to interpret the natural history. Grizzly sign most commonly found in the wild includes tracks, scats, dig sites, rubbing areas, and day beds. Less common sites include marked trees, wallows, excavated dens and kill sites. In my years of studying grizzlies in Alaska, I never

Fresh grizzly bear tracks along the Athabaska River in Jasper National Park (Alberta). Because of the wet sandy substrate, the tracks were well imprinted. The knife is 2.75 inches in length, so this was a mature bear.

Grizzly bear scat, early autumn (bistort roots and cow parsnip leaves). Knife is 4.75 inches in length. Scat containing berries is not so well formed, nor is scat discharged after consuming bloody meat.

observed a completely excavated and previously occupied den (although I found several dens started and abandoned). Generally I encountered only one or two kill sites each season, and these were always observed at a safe distance (hundreds of yards) with binoculars because of the extreme danger.

Grizzly bear tracks range considerably in size. The smaller tracks of a cub will normally be found in association with the tracks of a mature adult, the mother. These cub tracks are reasonable facsimiles, though miniaturized, of the adult track. Because of the extended foreclaws, adult grizzly tracks can be distinguished from the recurved foreclaw prints of black bears, with the grizzly claw marks extending as much as three inches in front of the toe prints of the front paws. Sometimes this is slightly more and sometimes this is slightly less, depending on the positioning of the paw, the gait of the animal (walking, loping, galloping) and the softness of the substrate. Tracks are best seen on mud, sand, or fresh wet snow. Also on the front tracks, the junction of the toes with the main pad forms a straighter line than with the black bear. The appearance of the grizzly track is more square than that of a black bear. Size is not a reliable indicator, as some black bears are extremely large and some grizzlies, especially subadults, are relatively small. Most of the hind tracks I measured in Denali measured between eight and eleven inches, with the majority averaging around nine inches. The front paws of adult grizzlies were generally around five inches wide at the widest span. Some were slightly larger. Elsewhere, as in Glacier National Park or Yellowstone National Park, the bears sometimes attain greater size than the subarctic populations and you may find the average figures proportionally higher. The best places to look for grizzly bear tracks are in the soft sands and muds along rivers and streams, in and around natural travel corridors such as canyons and passes, and along well-used trails. Grizzlies do maintain and utilize regular trails in the back country, as well as use those that humans make.

Along trails and across feeding sites you will find scat piles. These can assume a variety of sizes and shapes, and have diverse compositions depending on the season of the

A grizzly bear dig for alpine avens (*Dryas hookeriana*) about the 4000 foot level on Cathedral Mountain in Denali National Park. This dig, less than 24 hours old, was found while hiking in late June. Note camera tripod for scale. If you find a fresh dig site, always remain alert, as the bear or bears may still be in the area.

A small mammal (arctic ground squirrel) dig site near Destruction Bay, Kluane National Park, Yukon Territory.

Close up of a grizzly bear dig site. Knife indicates scale.

Close up of a grizzly bear small mammal dig site. Knife indicates scale.

year and the diet of the bear. Size is not a reliable indicator as to species, again because there are some very large black bears in the mountains of North America, as well as some less than mature grizzlies. Experts have suggested that any formed dropping with a diameter greater than 2.5 inches or a volume that exceeds 2.5 quarts can probably be considered indicative of grizzlies. My experience in the Alaska Range is consistent with this guideline. Grizzly bear scats are an important piece of sign, because they are incontrovertible evidence of what the bears are consuming. They literally come from the inside of the bear. Study them carefully, but remember that some wildlife vets advise extreme caution handling scat because of possible deseases. You will find, again depending on the time of year, roots, grasses, herbs, horsetail, partially digested large leaves, berries, the remnants of various mammals, pine cones, nuts, acorns, mushrooms, insect carapaces, and fish parts. The scat of a dry root or horsetail diet will generally be better formed than the diarrhetic scat of a blueberry or bloody carcass meal. Grizzly bears ingest hairs while grooming themselves and these can be found in scats. The hairs can then be studied by forensic specialists with microscopes to determine species. DNA specialists employ similar strategies in studying skin cells sloughed from the digestive tract. This is a very important technique for scientists attempting to determine grizzly presence or dispersal in areas such as the Cascade Mountains of Washington and Oregon, the Wind River Range of Wyoming, the Selway-Bitterroot Wilderness of Idaho, and the San Juan Mountains of Colorado.

Grizzly bear dig sites are found in those areas where the bears have turned over the sod or tundra in search roots, bulbs, tubers, and small mammals. These locations can be quite extensive, and cover many dozens of square yards. Early in the spring, these dig areas will often be at lower elevations, where the bears are excavating the nutritious roots of such plants as spring beauty, peavine, biscuitroot. It will appear as though someone with a gardener's shovel and a strong back has spent a couple of days tearing apart the turf. I have spent many hours in the cold windy days of May watching Alaska Range grizzlies systematically uproot every edible morsel from a

Grizzly bear den. As can be seen, the entrance is well concealed. Photograph by Adolph Murie. Courtesy of Arctic and Polar Regions Collection, University of Alaska.

Grizzly bear dig site for peavine. Photograph by Adolph Murie. Courtesy of Arctic and Polar Regions Collection, University of Alaska.

A wolf kill site along the East Fork of the Toklat River, Denali National Park. Note that the bull caribou carcass is uncovered.

A grizzly bear kill site on the Plains of Murie, Denali National Park. Note that the bull caribou carcass has been covered. Also note the large scat piles scattered near the carcass. Bear's stomach is swollen from having consumed so much meat.

Marked white spruce tree, Savage River, Denali National Park. Bears tear the bark off trees as a food source.

Grizzly bear hair attached to sap on marked white spruce tree.

streamside or river cutbank. The technique is as follows. The bear extends its forepaws, inserts its foreclaws in the soft ground, and then lurches backward, using the tremendous muscles of its frontquarters to rip out a sizeable chunk of ground. It then pulls the sod back, thus exposing the roots or tubers. Everything edible is consumed. After a morning or afternoon of this strenuous activity, the bears will become extremely dusty and dirty, and will sometimes retire to the stream or river to groom themselves. Later in the season, similarly configured dig sites will be found in the alpine regions, where the grizzlies dig for the roots of such favored plants as alpine bistort. In general, digging is thought to have important consequences for soil ecology and plant dispersal. Dig sites for small mammals are usually more confined, and deeper, than those for plants. I have come across small mammal digs that are two or three feet deep, with substantial rocks rolled aside and large amounts of topsoil excavated. While hunting caribou in 1992 in the Arctic National Wildlife Refuge, my partner (a biologist with the U.S.F.W.S.) and I came across a small mammal dig site that measured six feet by two feet by two feet. It literally appeared as though a back-hoe had been used as the bear attempted to gets its paws on the nutritious parka squirrel or marmot.

Rub areas are found in the spring and summer. These are locations where grizzlies remove their shedding coat by rubbing against rocks or rigid branches. Large amounts of hair can be found at these spots. The silver-tipped hair will have a characteristic ursine odor, and sometimes will be present in sizeable masses. These masses will give the appearance of sewing yarn scattered randomly through the alpine willows or aspen grove. Females with cubs sometimes shed their hair later in the summer than other members of the population, a biologist with the Alaska Game and Fish Department once told me, because their nutritional banks are drawn so low from lactating. Only later in the season do they have enough energy to grow the hairs which are, of course, made from protein.

Day beds are found at a greater distance from trails than other sign. They will generally be found only by those who leave officially designated trails and venture into the backcountry, which is not a recommended activity. In the Alaska Range, daybeds normally occupy an elevated location where the bear has a good view of its back-trail. Behind the daybed will be two or three escape routes that, if taken, afford the bear the opportunity to quickly disappear. Sows with cubs are particularly careful in their choice of daybeds. Daybeds on the tundra are excavated to conform with the shape of the bear's body. They are approximately three feet long, two feet wide, and one foot deep. All around the daybed will be scat piles, perhaps a way of indicating ownership as bears use the beds for several days before abandoning them. The daybed can also have grizzly bear hair in it, especially when the bears are shedding. I should mention that the word daybed is something of a misnomer, as bears will also rest in them at night. In the Alaska Range, sows with cubs often retire to their daybeds from around one in the morning to around six in the morning, the only time of day when the large males will usually venture into or through the active road corridor. This activity is especially noticeable during the June breeding season, when males roam widely in search of mates and once in a while will kill cubs (as do male African lions) in order to cause the female to become available for breeding purposes.

Grizzly bear dens are excavated at higher altitude areas where the grizzlies will be secure from predation or disturbance during the long winter months. Because of their secretive, isolated location, dens are extremely hard to find. The Craigheads discovered, in their historic study of the species in Yellowstone National Park, that grizzlies normally excavated their dens into a north-facing slope of around thirty to sixty degrees. Oftentimes these dens were dug under the roots of coniferous trees. Bears will also occupy natural caves. Whatever the case, grizzlies often drag in mosses, grasses or branches to make the beds more comfortable. In the arctic there are no trees, and finding safe denning locations is a problem for grizzlies. Because of the ubiquitous permafrost, the ground is frozen solid several feet beneath the surface. Excavation is impossible in such areas. Arctic grizzlies either find non-permafrost soils or occupy natural caverns or caves.

# 3
# A DARK, WOODED CAÑON

## *Grizzly Bear Habitat*

The grizzly, as I have said, does not seem to be much of a traveller. He generally, I believe, spends his life in a restricted area of country, and likes to live where he will not have to go far for food. He loves a dark, wooded cañon near good feeding grounds, and, winding across this cañon, his trails will be found. He is also fond of marshes where there is a stream and where the small willows grow thick and the grass heavy. Near the edge of such a stream he makes his bed, and here he lies up during the hot days of summer; and not very far away will be found the wallows where he has rolled in the mud to escape the flies. But a grizzly, when forced to, will travel far for the food he craves. He will go many miles to feed on berries during their season, if none grow near his own special haunts; and in the Bitter Roots [of Idaho] he makes considerable journeys to reach the salmon streams.

—William H. Wright, *The Grizzly Bear;*
*The Narrative of a Hunter-Naturalist*

As THE PIONEERING NATURALIST WILLIAM H. Wright observed, grizzly bears maintain a home range, and feed in different parts of that habitat as the seasons progress. Radiotracking has provided scientists with valuable knowledge as to habitat use. First, grizzly bear home ranges vary considerably in size, from relatively small in optimal habitat, such as Glacier National Park (estimated in 1974 at one bear per 8 square miles), to relatively large in less than optimal habitat, such as Gates of the Arctic National Park (estimated in 1982 at one bear per 57 square miles). Second, these home ranges and their respective food sources are deeply imprinted in the bear. When problem bears are anesthetized and translocated, they will often return to their home ranges within a matter of days or weeks. In October 1989, for example,

Spring habitat, valley of the Two Medicine River (northern Montana). Grizzlies from Glacier National Park descend to the valley of the Two Medicine in the spring, where they find the food resources so necessary to their survival.

Ridgetop glades are essential feeding areas for grizzlies. On this ridgetop in the Arctic National Wildlife Refuge grizzlies find low-bush cranberries, crowberries, bearberries, and blueberries, not to mention a thriving population of small mammals.

The transition from subalpine to alpine is rarely exact, as can be seen in this picture from Glacier National Park. The complex blending of climatic zones creates a rich habitat area for grizzlies, with abundant plant and animal food resources. This is the north-facing side of the mountain. Snow drifts linger longer on northern exposures, thus insuring ample vegetation when south-facing slopes have dried.

After-effects of massive forest fire along Laird River, Northwest Territories. Forest fires are natural events. They often have a beneficial effect for grizzlies by encouraging the growth of succulent vegetation and berry-producing plants previously suppressed by forest shade. Such plants are important for an omnivorous species like the grizzly.

Mixed coniferous and deciduous forest, along Peace River in northern British Columbia. In such diverse environments grizzlies find forests, meadows, swamps, bogs, muskeg, rivers, lakes, berry patches, and large and small mammals.

Mixed coniferous and deciduous forest surrounding St. Mary's Lake, Glacier National Park. This is some of the finest grizzly habitat in North America, with about one bear for every eight square miles of habitat. Note the extensive alplands in the background, where the grizzlies spend much of the summer.

Typical subalpine bear habitat in British Columbia's Stone Mountain Provincial Park. This rugged mountainous area just south of the Yukon Territory supports a good number of grizzlies, as well as caribou, moose, and a world-famous population of Stone Sheep.

Beaver pond, headwaters of Moose Creek near Denali. Grizzlies greatly benefit from beaver pond systems. These wetlands nurture sedges and berry-producing plants as well as attract prey species (ranging from ground squirrels to moose).

Alpine uplands, headwaters of Teklanika River in Alaska Range. Grizzlies are frequently observed in this region in the autumn, as they feast upon the plentiful blueberries, low-bush cranberries, and crow berries and as they hunt the rut-weakened bull caribou. Bears have denned in the high mountains in the background of this picture.

During the short summer, the alpine region hosts a vast number of wildflowers, a significant number of which are edible to grizzlies. Pictured here are mountain avens *(Dryas octopetala)*. Grizzlies dig for the roots of mountain avens, as was seen earlier in Chapter 2 (see photo of dig site on Cathedral Mountain). Photo taken in Alaska Range near Teklanika River headwaters.

Summertime and the living is easy. Here a mother grizzly and her two 3 year old cubs take a nap beside a series of springs. They had spent the morning feeding on the grass that flourished in this wet rich microsite. Photo taken near the headwaters of the McKinley River, Alaska Range.

Chandalar Shelf, near the headwaters of the Chandalar River, south slope of the Brooks Range, arctic Alaska. These broad passes are important habitat areas for arctic grizzlies, offering as they do significant populations of small mammals, carrion from wolf kills, and plentiful succulent vegetation.

Dall sheep feeding on cotton grass near the top of Atigun Pass, Brooks Range, arctic Alaska. Arctic grizzlies actively hunt Dall sheep during the spring lambing season.

Brooks Range in the Arctic National Wildlife Refuge, timberline can be low as 2300 feet. A hundred miles to the north, near the heads of rivers such as the Canning and Sheenjek, there are no trees at all.

In this section you will find photographs grouped by climatic zone, each indicating some of those ecological land units (ELUs) of importance to grizzlies. An ELU is a particular geographic area with a unique assemblage of vegetation, soils and landforms. For example, a glacial cirque basin ELU is defined by grizzly bear ecologist John Craighead as "being characterized by flat, boulder-strewn slab rock with approximately 50 percent exposed rock surface and 50 percent soil-covered surface." The soil is "shallow except in crevices and swalls where rooting depth is sufficient to support turf and, rarely, krummholz." What are of key importance in all the ELUs found in grizzly habitat are the microsites—those even smaller areas containing large amounts of criti-cally important food. These microsites can include such areas as root beds, berry patches, whitebark pine ridges, ungulate calving areas, trout and salmon streams, moth sites, and active warm-water springs. Scientists are de-veloping sophisticated methods, primarily employing LANDSAT satellite images, to accurately map and eval-uate these sites, as well as other aspects of grizzly habi-tat (denning sites, availability of cover, surface water), so that more informed management decisions can be made. John Craighead has been among the most active researchers in developing these new techniques, with extensive field work having been done by his team in the Lincoln Scapegoat Wilderness Area of northern Mon-tana and the Gates of the Arctic National Park in north-ern Alaska. It was John Craighead, together with his brother Frank and others such as Maurice Hornocker, who undertook a seminal long-term study of grizzly populations and habitat use in Yellowstone National Park from 1959 through 1970. Their 1966 *National Geo-graphic* television special introduced the nation to the secret world of the grizzly.

One of the best ways to familiarize yourself with griz-zly habitat is to hike (or drive) from the lowlands to the uplands. In this way you gradually pass through the three major climatic zones, and can note the subtle changes in landforms and vegetation. There are a variety of places where this can be undertaken. In Glacier National Park, for example, you can drive from St. Mary Lake, which is a valley bottom surrounded by grass shrublands and temperate woodlands of spruce, fir and aspen, through the fir forests of the subalpine zone, to the top of Logan Pass, with the treeless tundra of the alpine zone. The lower elevations represent valuable spring habitat areas, with winter-killed carcasses, early-greening grass and horsetail, over-wintered berries, and various root beds. The subalpine represents a habitat exploited throughout the season when snows were abscent. The alpine constitutes a summer and early autumn habitat with a particularly rich complement of succulent vegetation and berries.

Another strategy would be to descend in altitude from a higher to a lower elevation, pursuing a route similar to that which a grizzly follows after leaving the den. In Yellowstone, this could be accomplished by hiking from the vicinity of Mount Washburn, a high elevation area offering denning possibilities, toward Hayden Valley, which is essential summer habitat for grizzlies. In doing so, you would pass from the climatically inhospitable alpine zone to a more temperate region of the park, replete with hot springs. A final possibility, in Denali National Park, would be to hike west from the spruce forest along the Teklanika River four miles to the base of Cathedral Mountain, and then climb upward a mile or so into the alpine zone. This would take you from essential spring habitat in the Teklanika lowlands to critical autumn berry habitat and winter denning areas in the alpine zone. This could also be accomplished in Denali along the Savage River by climbing Primrose Ridge just to the west, a hike I've made several times for the very purpose of more intimately familiarizing myself with grizzly habitat.

Whichever hike, or drive, you choose, one thing is certain. You will come away from the experience duly impressed with the spectacular beauty of grizzly bear habitat. Grizzlies occupy some of the most wild and rugged country on the continent. I often think that one of the reasons that I have devoted so many years of my life to studying the species is that I love so much the country in which they live.

## THE TEMPERATE CLIMATIC ZONE

The temperate climatic zone is the one you first see when driving into the mountains. These are the lowland areas—foothills and valley floors—directly associated with the higher mountains. Generally you will notice more dry, grassy vegetation at lower elevations. There will also be more open-canopied woodlands. At the temperate latitudes of Yellowstone and Grand Teton National Parks, sunny coniferous groves impart to the landscape the pleasant appearance of a cultivated parkland. It is to these lowland areas that grizzlies gravitate in the spring, when snows are still deep in the subalpine and alpine climatic zones where they denned. Here in the temperate climatic zone the hungry bears find winter-killed ungulates, emerging small mammal populations, insects, overwintered berries, greening grass, horsetail, and the nutritious roots of plants such as spring beauty and peavine. Later in the spring, the newly born young of moose, elk and deer become available in the foothills and valleys as well. Many of the best spawning streams are found in this zone, and offer grizzlies the opportunity to fish during the summer months for salmon and trout, depending on availability. Here, too, grizzlies often come in the mid to late autumn, when rutting bull moose and elk are more vulnerable to predation, and when early snows may have already covered food sources in the highlands.

The upper boundary of the temperate climatic zone varies considerably by latitude, as do the vegetational associations. In the grizzly habitat of southern Colorado (last confirmed grizzly: 1979), you would find the following in the temperate zone: Gambel oak woodlands (a source of acorns for bears), piñon-juniper woodlands (piñon nuts are a nutritious bear food), cottonwood groves, Ponderosa pine woodlands, and prickly pear cactus fruit (edible to humans and grizzlies) on some south-facing slopes. None of these species, except perhaps colonial cottonwoods, would be present in the subalpine or alpine climatic zones. Farther north, in Yellowstone and the upper Rockies, John Craighead has defined the upper boundary of the temperate zone as beginning where Douglas fir trees are replaced by whitebark pine trees.

In the subarctic regions of Canada and the Alaska, the temperate climatic zone would conform with the foothills and valley floor regions vegetated with white spruce, quaking aspen, and cottonwood. Because of the permafrost, which keeps the ground permanently wet, the subarctic has none of the dry grasslands and shrublands found in the temperate zone of the Rockies. The river bottoms and foothills, however, are still used identically by the resident grizzlies. In the spring, bears actively hunt there for moose calves, dig for peavine roots, chase small mammals around, graze the emerging patches of grass and horsetail, and eat overwintered blueberries, soapberries and bear berries. These areas are also important in the summer months, when searun salmon finish their annual migration in the lowland rivers. Each July, for example, many of the road-corridor grizzlies of Denali National Park dissappear for a week or so as they migrate twenty-five miles north to Toklat Springs to fish for dog salmon. Similarly, grizzlies are found in this more temperate lower Toklat River region in the late fall when bull moose weakened by the rut are killed by wolves.

The temperate climatic zone is both an important climatic zone for grizzlies and, because of its accessibility, the area most in conflict with human activities. In his intensive vegetational study of the Lincoln-Scapegoat Wilderness in Montana, John Craighead quantified the plant food sources (based on calories) in all three climatic zones, and assigned the temperate zone an over-all score of 29 (with 28 for the subalpine and 12 for the alpine). Craighead used LANDSAT photographs to completely map and study the research area, with assistants combing the field to verify the plants. In the past, developers of ski resorts, timber projects, second home developments, golf courses, and mining operations, while quite often environmentally consciousness, have perhaps failed to fully appreciate the impact of their activities on wildlife, especially grizzlies. Public land man-

Even in the subarctic, there is a region analogous to the temperate climatic zone. Here, in the valley of the Savage River,
grizzlies gather every spring to dig for the roots of peavine, feed
on over-wintered bearberries and blueberries, and hunt for
new-born moose calves. As can be seen here, their summer
habitat just a few miles up the Savage River is still covered in
snow. Photo was taken May 3rd in a year of average snow.
Male bears and subadult bears were already active, but females
and cubs did not appear for ten to fourteen more days.

agers and leaders in the private sector now have the data
to make more informed decisions as to how to best shep-
erd human activities on a landscape with such a widely
roaming species as the grizzly.

## THE SUBALPINE CLIMATIC ZONE

The subalpine climatic zone is gradually entered as
you hike or motor from the lowlands into the highlands.
If you are driving in Yellowstone National Park from the
Lamar River Valley toward Hayden Valley, for example,
you will eventually leave the lodgepole-Douglas fir parkland behind and climb into the whitebark pine and subalpine fir groves. The subalpine climatic zone will be
entered gradually. Here is a realm of thick forests and
open clearings. This cool moist environment is perfect
for growing berries, and it is in the subalpine that many
of the grizzly's most important berry foods, especially
huckleberries, are found. A second major food item is
the nut of the whitebark pine. These lovely broad-
crowned trees are abundant throughout the northwest-

ern U.S. and California, as well as in Alberta and British Columbia. John Craighead reported a particular Yellowstone grizzly consuming nuts during a particularly good year gained 3.6 pounds per day on the diet.

Rocky Mountain grizzlies often spend much of the summer and early fall in the subalpine zone, harvesting a broad array of berries, gobbling up whitebark pine nuts, fishing when possible (as with the spawning trout of Yellowstone), hunting small mammals, and tearing apart fallen logs for insects. During the autumn, bears will hunt rutting moose and elk in the subalpine zones of the Rockies as conditions warrant. The bears may also utilize the upper reaches of the subalpine (rocky palisades, avalanche chutes) during the winter months for dens. The subalpine zone in the frostier latitudes of northern Canada and Alaska is functionally the same in its relationship to grizzlies. Though the whitebark pine is abscent in the subarctic, berry production, especially of blueberries and low-bush cranberries, is high. Small mammals are abundant, and caribou replace elk as the meat source. Grizzlies sometimes find wolf-killed caribou in the areas below timberline where wolves often hunt, and wolves often lose carcasses to insistent grizzlies.

One of the chief human conflicts in the subalpine occurs during the summer with wilderness fishing camps and in the autumn with hunting camps. Many of these conflicts are centered around the cook tent where human food is prepared. In October 1994 I was able to observe an experiment conducted by the Montana Game and Fish Department that may help to alleviate this chronic source of grizzly mortality. The experiment took place on the Pine Butte Grizzly Bear Preserve, that is administered by the Nature Conservancy. The 18,000-acre Pine Butte preserve protects a large swamp adjoining the Rocky Mountain Front. This is the last portion of prairie utilized by grizzly bears in North America, and is critical habitat for grizzlies in the spring. In the experiment a dead horse was placed inside a small electrified fence. Cameras monitored grizzly response to the fence. The experiment was a success. No grizzlies were successful in reaching the food source. Eventually the fence was removed and the bears were permitted to feed. Authorities

Englemann spruce forest in South San Juan Wilderness (southern Colorado). A 16 year old female grizzly was killed just west of here in 1979. Note the sidehill parks on the opposite side of the canyon wall. Here the grizzlies historically found succulent vegetation, berries, and small mammal populations.

are now seriously considering electrifying all cook tents in the Bob Marshall Wilderness Area with mobile electrical units. If implemented, this system could offer the bears, and people, a greater measure of security. A second major source of conflict in the subalpine occurs when ski resorts are built or expanded. This inevitably effects travel corridors, feeding areas, and denning locations, and leads to the degradation of down-valley areas developed to support the facility.

The grizzly bear can often be found in the alpine climatic zone—the area above treeline—by early summer. At that time the snows have receded, and many of the green plants utilized in the lower canyons and river bottoms during the spring are again appearing at higher elevations. These include grasses, horsetail, spring beauty and numerous others. Over-wintered berries are available in the alpine region as the snows recede, as well as burgeoning small mammal populations. These remote upland areas are also sometimes used by moose, wild sheep, elk, and deer as birthing areas, thus providing another food source. Grizzlies wander far and wide over the alpine through the summer and well into the autumn, particularly after blueberries become available. Their movements are by no means random, but are locked into plant location and plant phenology (the different times and places at which plants become available for eating, which vary by altitude). The bears may remain in the alpine until declining availability of food leads them to descend to other areas, where they seek such food items as whitebark pine nuts (in the northern Rockies), late-running salmon (in northern Alaska on the upper Tanana River), and rut-weakened ungulates (moose, elk) prior to denning. Denning locations are sometimes found in the alpine or close to the alpine, especially near avalanche chutes where their security is enhanced by inaccessibility. Grizzlies living in the arctic (see next section) spend their entire lifetimes in this climatic zone, and must roam over large home ranges in order to survive in such a depauperate environment.

In the alpine region, vegetation has adapted to the severe environment—short growing season, cold temperatures, thin air (south of the true arctic), and intense sunlight—by utilizing fascinating strategies. Plants grow tightly packed and close to the ground to avoid the wind. Epidermal hairs and scales are resistant to desiccation and also reflect sunlight. Most of the plants are perennials that flower and disperse seeds and fruits quickly in the brief summer. In coarse soil and rock fields, lichens—always an indicator of the health of an ecosystem because of their sensitivity to acids—grow on the

Headwaters of Athabasca River, Jasper National Park (Alberta).
Much of this park is in the subalpine climatic zone. In its 2.7
million acres a large population of grizzlies roam. In the dense
forests near the Athabasca River grizzlies feast on whitebark
pine nuts and huckleberries.

surface of the country rock. Boulder fields may have few
vascular plants, but they afford protection for families of
marmots, ground squirrels and other small mammals.
Protected ravines support moisture-loving plants like
saxifrage and bluebells, and blueberries can grow ex-
tensively here and elsewhere. On the dry, wind-swept
ridges, short-stemmed cushion plants like moss campion
and alpine forget-me-not form a dense carpet. Hiking in
these areas, you are often struck by the fragility of life in

such an extreme environment and how noble is the struggle for life where it occurs.

One good thing about the alpine region is that grizzly bears are more easily seen. There is often little or no cover, except in marshy areas or headwaters filled with willows, and bears can sometimes be seen for miles. This is especially true in the spring after the snows have melted and before the country has greened up, and again in the autumn after the alpine willow and dwarf birch leaves have dropped and before the snows have returned. Look first for movement and second for shape—the circular or round body of a bear. Late in the summer the fur of grizzlies in the alpine may become sunbleached, so you might particularly concentrate on a brighter pattern against the less colorful earth tones. Grizzly bears above timberline can be seen digging for marmots, uprooting beds of alpine bistort, sleeping on snowbanks to escape mosquitoes, gobbling up gallons of blueberries, playing on the edge of glacial tarns, licking up hatches of army cutworm moths, or chasing the young caribou.

## THE ARCTIC HABITAT REGION

The Arctic is treated as a separate section because of the profound differences, climatically and geographically, between this austere environment, which occupies the northernmost regions of Alaska, the Yukon Territory, and the Northwest Territories, and the rest of North America. Technically, the arctic is said to begin north of latitude 66 degrees 33 minutes, but I prefer to think of the arctic as being that polar country beyond the furthest upright trees. Along the Dalton Highway in Alaska, a road that runs from Fairbanks to Prudhoe Bay on the Arctic Ocean, the Artic Circle (66 degrees 33 minutes) is crossed at mile 115.3, but upright trees continue to grow along the road for another 121.5 miles to milepost 236.8 at the base of the Chandalar Shelf. I never feel as though I am in the arctic until I have left the last white spruce and aspen behind and reached the headwaters of the Chandalar River. To me the treeless tundra, the vast expanses devoid of upright vegetation, is the essence of the arctic and of the realm of the arctic grizzly.

The severity of the arctic climate, and the paucity of

Subalpine riparian habitat, Banff National Park (Alberta).
Formed in 1887, Banff was Canada's first National Park. Along
these upland streams, grizzlies can often be seen in the late
summer and early autumn, harvesting what the Canadians call
buffalo berries (Shcpherdia canadensis) and hunting the ground
squirrels and marmots.

Subalpine forest, Kananaskis Country, Alberta. In this heavily-
timbered wildland south of Banff National Park (Alberta), grizzlies are often seen in the spring grazing on grass in the
south-facing meadows, as are pictured here.

food sources as compared to the temperate latitudes, makes life difficult for all animals. Because of their large daily food requirements, grizzlies are particularly challenged. First, there is little cover, which means the bears are exposed to the elements, especially the wind, and to their major predators, consisting of other bears, humans and wolves. Second, there are shorter periods of food availability. In Yellowstone National Park, grizzlies begin to appear as early as March, but in the Arctic grizzlies are sometimes not seen until late May. Snows come earlier at the high latitudes, and bears must enter their dens no later than the second week in October, whereas grizzlies at lower latitudes sometimes remain active through November and in mild winters even through December. Third, because the habitat is so depauperate, grizzlies must have much larger home ranges. Fourth, the arctic grizzly has a very low reproductive potential, and populations can quickly be lost if mortality significantly exceeds natality. The bears do not become sexually mature until their sixth summer (and sometimes longer), whereas grizzlies elsewhere can become sexually active in their fourth or fifth summer; litters tend to be smaller with greater cub mortality; the reproductive interval is longer; and there is a shorter period of reproductive potential. Also, the bear populations are extremely scattered, and this low density hinders the social contacts necessary to the breeding process. Fifth, the process of denning can be tricky in permafrost, as the soil is often unstable, there are no trees into whose root systems dens can be dug, and natural caves offering the right exposure and protection are difficult to find.

All of this means that arctic grizzlies are living on the margins, and that only a few factors changed could result in their extirpation or extinction. Although it is probably true that development of the coastal oil and gas in the Arctic National Wildlife Refuge would not directly impact many grizzlies, the indirect effects could be significant. First, the Porcupine caribou herd could lose both the sensitive calving area and the coastal insect relief areas; these caribou are an important food source to the arctic grizzlies of northeastern Alaska and the northwestern Yukon. Second, the development would defi-

Arctic plain, north slope of the Brooks Range, looking south over the Saganavirtok River. Arctic grizzlies descend to these lowland areas in the spring, much as their cousins in the Rockies visit lower valleys during the same season. In the fall the arctic grizzlies return to the high mountains to harvest berries and hunt for the rut-weakened caribou and moose.

nitely result in increased sport hunting and in increased poaching of the grizzlies. It is possible that one of the reasons the Central Arctic caribou herd has increased since the pipeline was built in 1975, is that the chief predators—wolves and grizzlies—have been either eliminated or greatly reduced in number through both sport hunting and poaching. The same could be true for the Porcupine caribou herd if the coastal plain is developed without a concern for the environment and for proper law enforcement.

For years the arctic habitat region was accessible only to those willing to fly in single-engine Piper Supercubs and Cessna float planes. In 1994, however, the Alaska Supreme Court ruled that the general public must have access to the 450-mile gravel access road, the Dalton Highway, from Fairbanks through the Brooks Range to Prudhoe Bay on the Arctic Ocean. (One of my former graduate students, Mike Jensen, has written the first guidebook to the Dalton Highway, published by Epicenter Press and distributed by Graphic Arts in Portland,

Oregon). Those interested in observing and studying the arctic grizzly now have ample opportunity to do so. There is no rifle hunting permitted for five miles on either side of the road, and so the road corridor has become a *de facto* park, with grizzly sightings common. The best area to observe arctic grizzlies is around the Chandalar Shelf, at the headwaters of the Chandalar River, and on Atigun Pass, where there are also large numbers of Dall sheep. Further north, massive herds of caribou can be observed in early August as they migrate from their summer grounds on the arctic coastal plain to their wintering grounds south of the Brooks Range. Grizzlies and wolves can be seen in association with this mass migration, which is the largest such assemblage of wild animals left on earth.

# 4
# EVERYTHING BUT GRANITE
## *Grizzly Bear Plant Food*

To him almost every thing is food except granite. Every tree helps to feed him, every bush and herb, with fruits and flowers, leaves and bark; and all the animals he can catch—badgers, gophers, ground squirrels, lizards, snakes, and ants, bees, wasps, old and young, together with their eggs and larvae and nests. Crauched and hashed, down all go to his marvelous stomach, and vanish as if cast into a fire. What digestion! A sheep or a wounded deer or a pig he eats warm, about as quickly as a boy eats a buttered muffin; or should the meat be a month old, it still is welcomed with tremendous relish. After so gross a meal as this, perhaps the next will be strawberries and clover, or raspberries with mushrooms and nuts, or puckery acorns and chokecherries.

—John Muir, "Bears"

BECAUSE GRIZZLY BEARS ARE AN OMNIVOROUS species, their study affords the opportunity to learn about plants. In educating myself about grizzlies, I found the study of bear plant foods to be the most enjoyable task. First of all, the plants are often strikingly beautiful, especially in their flowering period. Secondly, we humans can eat many of the plants that bears do, especially the berries. It's probably not incorrect to assume that as ancient human populations spread through North America, they closely watched bears to learn what wild plants were edible. Many of these plants grow in all three climatic zones and are available at different times of the year as the summer progresses.

The greatest surprise of my first summer in the Alaskan Range was seeing bears graze for hours on grass (*Arc-*

tagrostis sp.) and the more primitive plant, horsetail (*Equisetum arvense*). Both plants were found in early spring on south-facing terrain near the Toklat River and other major drainages. Frankly, I had expected more carcass-scavenging and opportunistic hunting in the spring. Both of these activities were spontaneously pursued, but it was plant foraging that most preoccupied the bears. I would not have believed it possible if I had not seen it with my own two eyes. At a distance, the grizzlies literally appeared to be cattle grazing in a pasture. I was curious as to the nutritional value of grass and horsetail. A park naturalist informed me that, before grasses channel their energy into flower and seed production, they have fairly high crude protein levels. The same is true of horsetail. As adaptations to this largely vegetable diet, bears have large crushing molars and the longest intestinal length relative to body size of any carnivore. They are poor digesters of cellulose, the naturalist said, but when there is nothing else to eat, grass is better than starving.

In the spring grizzlies also utilize many other plant resources, including roots and bulbs. One of the most important is spring beauty (*Claytonia lanceolata*). This lovely flowering plant is found from the Sheenjek River of the Arctic National Wildlife Refuge south thousands of miles into the canyons of the Navajo River in southern Colorado. It has nutritious corms and an edible taproot. Another important rooted plant of the subarctic is peavine (*Hedysarum alpinum*). Grizzlies will spend hours digging for peavine roots in the soft, sandy loam of the river bottoms. In the Rocky Mountains biscuitroot (*Lomatium ambiguum*) is a popular spring food of the lower elevations, especially on dry south-facing hills. The leaves smell something like parsley and scientists believe grizzlies locate biscuitroot plants partly through scent. Another rooted plant located by scent is the widespread wild onion (*Allium cernuum*).

Gradually other plants begin to grow and make themselves available for eating. These include such leafy plants as clover (*Orthocarpus tenuifolius*), dandelion (*Taraxacum officinale*), fireweed (*Epilobium latifolium*), Saxifrage (*Boykinia richardsonii*), cow parsnip (*Heracleum lana-*

Grizzlies consume horsetail *(Equisetum arvense)* in the early spring when other food sources are unavailable.

Grizzlies will graze for hours on grass. The grass here is *Arctagrostis latifolium*. The yellow flower is the yellow marsh saxifrage *(Saxifraga hirculus)* and is also consumed by grizzlies.

A grizzly bear sow digging for peavine *(Hedysarum alpinum)*. Her two spring cubs are learning to eat peavine roots for the first time.

Four grizzly bear favorites (clockwise from upper left): peavine, dock, alpine bistort, and blueberries.

This grizzly has ventured up into the alpine while the snow-banks are still abundant. The only thing she has found to eat are the roots and branches of alpine willow (Salix sp.). Interestingly enough, willow contains high amounts of sali-cyclic acid, which is the active ingredient in commercial as-pirin. The Eskimos made an herbal tea from the bark and leaves.

Grizzlies consume the leaves of cow parsnip (Heracleum lana-tum), with the large white umbels, and fireweed (Epilobium augustifolium), with the red flowers.

Bear Flower *(Boykinia richardsonii)* is consumed by grizzlies,
white flowers and all, as are, in the foreground, bluebells
*(Mertensia ciliata)* and fireweed *(Epilobium augustifolium)*.

A grizzly bear digging for the roots of the alpine bistort *(Polygonum bistortoides)* far above timberline.

Mushrooms, such as the Chanterelle, are eaten by grizzlies, especially in wet seasons when they are more common. The reddish leaves are of blueberry *(Vaccinium uliginosum)* and alpine bearberry *(Arctostaphylus alpina)*, both essential berries for grizzly bears. Do not eat mushrooms, or any plant, unless you have expert help in identification.

Grizzly cub eating soapberry *(Shepherdia canadensis)*. If you look closely you can see the small red berries of the soapberry plant to the right (your right) of the cub. Dwarf birch is the orange-leafed plant directly behind him and the yellow-leafed plant to the left is alpine willow. The soapberry, also known as the buffaloberry, is an extremely important food source to the grizzly in the autumn.

Soapberry up close.

The mother of the grizzly cub in the photo at left is also eating soapberries. The feeding technique is to take the entire branch into the mouth and strip the berries off forcefully with the tongue, ingesting a few leaves and twigs as well. Grizzlies will do this for hours and hours in the autumn.

Both grizzly bears and black bears will consume rose hips, particularly in good years when they are fat and plentiful. Rose hips are often found in old burn areas in association with wild raspberries *(American Red Raspberry)* and high-bush cranberries *(Viburnum edule)*. All three are consumed by grizzlies.

*tum*), and Sourdock (*Rumex arcticus*). Where available, grizzlies will also eat whitebark pine nuts beginning in the spring, and this will continue through the season. Later in the summer, when the bears are in the alpine climatic zone, they dig for the roots of alpine bistort (*Polygonum bistortoides*). Like many of the others, bistort is a plant I have observed in the southern Rockies, Canadian Rockies, and various mountains ranges of Alaska. In Colorado it has a white flower and in Alaska it has a pink flower, but it is still the same plant and in both places an ideal grizzly bear food. The starchy rootstock can be as thick as a good-sized carrot. Another good food of the higher and lower elevations is sedge (*Carex sp.*). These plants favor boggy areas near springs, streams, and standing water and are a staple of grizzlies, whether in Yellowstone or Denali.

Berries are among the favored late summer and autumn foods of grizzlies. Over-wintered berries are also consumed during the early spring, when other high-energy food sources are scarce. Oftentimes in the spring, the bears are on a fairly restricted diet of horsetail and grass, and the addition of the berries is no doubt welcome, both in terms of energy and taste. In years when berries are scarce, normally because of drought but also when catastrophic events such as forest fires or freak, high-country blizzards occur, bear populations can become severely stressed. As a result, conflicts with people sometimes increase, as the bears become so desparate for food they seek sources they ordinarily avoid. At such times it becomes clear just how important the annual berry crop is in the yearly life of the grizzly. The bears rely on the berries to bulk-up for the long winter sleep during which they consume no food and must rely on body fat in order to survive. It is probably not a coincidence that bear and berries have the same root word, the Old English *bher*, which means to give birth.

The berry I most associate with the grizzly is the blueberry (*Vaccinium sp.*), probably because I have watched for so many hours as they gobbled them up. In a good berry season, Alaskan grizzlies will spend days, even weeks, in the best berry patches. At this time of year their muzzles can actually become stained blue from eating so many berries. Other berries of the high mountain regions that are important to grizzlies include crowberry (*Empetrum Nigrum*), soapberry (*Shepherdia canadensis*, also known as buffaloberry), bearberry (*Arctostaphylus alpina*), and low-bush cranberry (*Vaccinium vitis*). These berry plants are found in one form or another throughout the range of the grizzly. Both wild strawberries (*Fragaria vesca*) and wild raspberries (*Rubus parviflorus*), ordinarily found in stream drainages, are also widespread and regularly consumed by grizzlies.

In learning more about grizzly bear plant foods, I would recommend any one of a number of books. *Guide to Rocky Mountain Wildflowers*, by John and Frank Craighead and Ray Davis first published in 1963 (Houghton Mifflin), is still in print and quite authoritative. The guide is indispensable to those studying grizzlies in Wyoming, Montana, Idaho, Washington, and southern Alberta and British Columbia. Adolph Murie's *The Grizzly Bears of Mount McKinley* (University of Washington Press, 1974) is the single best guide to the eating habits of interior Alaskan grizzlies. Murie's empirical findings would be applicable to any non-coastal Alaska grizzly populations, and would also apply to the Yukon, the Northwest Territories, and northern British Columbia and Alberta. Various national or provincial park naturalists can suggest other, more specific guides as necessary. Remember that it is illegal to gather plant specimens in parks.

Once you are in the park, I would highly recommend that you take a day hike with one of the park naturalists. Every park has regularly scheduled hikes into the backcountry that are guided by experienced park personnel. These can range from a one-hour discovery hike to an all-day excursion to a mountaintop. This is probably the single, best way to learn about the plants and their relationship to the grizzly. One morning on the trail with an expert can teach you more than weeks of stumbling around by yourself with a guidebook. Remember to take a lot of photographs. In this way you can make your own reference guide at home, and more quickly learn the plants.

A final suggestion is to take an informal botany course, such as are offered increasingly at wilderness ranches and lodges, parks and preserves. These intensive courses in mountain botany are normally taught by university professors or trained naturalists. Camp Denali and North Face Lodge at Wonder Lake in Denali National Park both offer such courses. In Jackson Hole, Wyoming the Teton School offers a number of courses. The Pine Butte Grizzly Preserve near Choteau, Montana also offers a wide selection of natural history courses. Grizzly bear expert Dr. Charles Jonkel teaches frequently at Pine Butte, as does Dr. James Halfpenny at the Teton School. Yellowstone and Glacier National Parks also have summer institutes. Whatever your choice as to a mode of further education on the subject, I'm sure you will find the process as much fun as I did.

# 5

# THE RUSH OF THE GREAT BEAR

## Grizzly Bear Animal Food

An old hunter who a dozen years ago wintered at Jackson Lake, in northwestern Wyoming, told me that when the snows got deep on the mountains the moose came down and took their abode near the lake, on its western side. Nothing molested them during the winter. Early in the spring a grizzly came out of its den, and he found their tracks in many places, as it roamed restlessly about, evidently very hungry. Finding little to eat in the bleak, snow-drifted woods, it soon began to depredate on the moose, and killed two or three, generally by lying in wait and dashing out on them as they passed near its lurking-place. Even the bulls were at that season weak, and of course hornless, with small desire to fight; and in each case the rush of the great bear—doubtless made with the ferocity and speed which so often belie the seeming awkwardness of the animal—bore down the startled victim, taken utterly unawares before it had a chance to defend itself.

—Theodore Roosevelt, "Old Ephraim, the Grizzly Bear"
Hunting Trips of a Ranchman

ALTHOUGH THE GRIZZLY BEAR IS PRIMARILY A vegetarian, meat protein comprises an important part of the annual diet. This meat can include a variety of sources such as carrion, fish, and small and large mammals. Bears acquire meat through fishing, active hunting, scavenging winter-killed carcasses, and preempting the carcasses of other predators. A large mammal carcass claimed by a grizzly bear is normally covered or partially buried under a pile soil, branches, and plant debris. A word of caution: if you ever come upon one of these meat hoards, immediately depart the area, though not of course at a run. Few things are more valuable to a grizzly bear than several hundred pounds of fresh or fetid meat. In June 1972, while exploring a few hundred yards from a

As with caribou and moose, bull elk are hunted by grizzlies in the fall after the rut. In Yellowstone, elk calves form a significant part of grizzly diet in the spring.

Bison range wild in Yellowstone National Park and furnish an occasional meal for grizzlies. Once wolves are restored to the park (1995), the number of carcasses available for grizzlies should increase.

Yellowstone picnic ground where my family had stopped for lunch, I stumbled upon the buried carcass of a four-point bull elk. I poked around the unusual discovery for several minutes before realizing what it was (I was 18 and fresh from Ohio). Needless to say, I was extremely lucky not to have been confronted by the owner of the meat. Others have not been. Be forewarned and be careful. In 1986, at the Fate of the Grizzly Conference in Boulder, Colorado, grizzly ecologist Dr. John Craighead was asked the following question by a member of the audience: "If you accidentally run into a grizzly kill-site, what sort of steps should you take?" His answer: "Big ones."

The two best times of year to observe grizzly predation of large mammals are in spring and autumn. In spring the resident ungulates (moose, wild sheep, caribou, deer, elk, antelope) are giving birth. For a brief period of time the young have not yet developed full escape speed in their leg muscles and are vulnerable to predation. Studies have shown that Yellowstone National Park grizzlies are particularly active hunters of elk calves at this time of the year, which runs from late May to early June. This is the most visible hunting all year. In the autumn, just before denning, male ungulates such as bull moose and bull elk are weakened from the rut (breeding season). For several weeks the males of these species constantly defend and mate with their harem cows. Sometimes the bulls eat only sporadically. Consequently, the most active herd bulls lose valuable weight and strength. This sometimes renders them easy targets for wolves and bears, especially after the first snows fall and the exhausted bulls are less mobile and more stressed by the cold. Wildlife viewing at this time of the year can be complicated by early blizzards and closing of park roads. All in all, spring is probably the best time.

Those who have witnessed grizzly predation describe it in a number of different ways. One mode of attack is to charge or chase the target animal, whether it is an elk or a caribou, and grab it from the rear. After pulling the prey down, the victim's neck is broken in a powerful bite or the throat is destroyed in a similar fashion. Montana cinematographer Bob Landis filmed an incident on the Teklanika River in Denali, in which a sow grizzly

New born wild sheep lambs are hunted by grizzlies in the spring. These are Dall sheep on Primrose Ridge in Denali National Park. Further to the south are Stone sheep (British Columbia) and Rocky Mountain bighorn sheep.

Alaskan Wolf along Toklat River. Grizzlies periodically pre-empt wolf kill sites, thus securing large amounts of protein.

Red fox are often observed around grizzly bear kill sites, sharing in the meat.

After spawning, sea-run salmon die by the hundreds in their headwater rivers and streams. Even grizzlies living a thousand miles from the ocean can benefit from this important protein source.

successfully killed a bull caribou previously injured by wolves. When the large-antlered bull, standing beside the river, spotted the advancing bear he assumed a last-stand defensive posture, with his legs widely planted and his massive rack deployed forward. At that point the sow galloped directly for the bull, which was bleeding visibly from the hindquarters. A few feet from the bull the sow suddenly stopped, studied him for a moment from several different angles, and then lunged between the antlers for the spinal cord. The spine was severely injured with a crushing bite. Afterwards the bear, joined by her two cubs, dragged the still-kicking caribou into the river and drowned him. They reportedly fed on him for several days. Still other observers have reported grizzlies using a forepaw in a sudden head slap to knock an animal down. Wolves can employ somewhat different predatory strategies. Denali ranger Bill McDonald, who was based at the Sanctuary River patrol cabin for two summers, told me of a large wolf on the East Fork of the Toklat (the alpha male of the local pack, as a matter of fact) that ran a bull caribou to death over a period of three days, never permitting the bull to rest and keeping it constantly on the move. When the bull was finally fatigued and momentarily distracted, the wolf lunged for the kill. Grizzlies, with their greater body weight, would find such a prolonged marathon impossible.

In six years of observing grizzlies in the Alaska Range, Brooks Range, and Kenai Peninsula, I never saw a grizzly successfully hunt and kill a large mammal. I did videotape and photograph a number of unsuccessful stalks and charges. In each case, the object of the hunt was an isolated caribou that appeared to fit in one or more of the following categorics: below normal weight, below normal strength, confused, injured by prior accident or wolf attack, female, calf or subadult male, caught by surprise. I never saw a grizzly attempt to kill a Dall sheep or a moose. Dall sheep inhabit rough terrain that often forces predators to rely on ambush strategies. Mature moose are the largest animals of the north country and, if healthy and not affected by the rut, are difficult for a grizzly to kill. Several times a season I observed grizzlies hunt and kill parka squirrels or marmots, which they

Small mammals, such as this ground squirrel, are eaten regularly by grizzlies.

immediately ate. Parka squirrels and other small mammals, researchers have found, provide the grizzly with a number of valuable nutrients and minerals. In one particularly humorous incident, I watched a mother grizzly chase down and kill a parka squirrel, only to have the squirrel stolen by one of her cubs, who gobbled the treat down before the mother could react. Needless to say, he was severely punished for this misdeed, a somewhat violent scene watched intently by his twin sister.

What was far more common was to observe a grizzly feeding from the carcass of a large mammal (moose, Dall sheep, caribou), the kill evidently having been accomplished by the bear or by wolves during the twilight or dark hours. Another not infrequent scene, especially in June, was to observe wolves and grizzlies fight over possession of a carcass. It was never clear who had done the killing, though I suspect wolves, being full-time professional hunters, had probably accomplished the feat. I never saw a grizzly lose a fight with a wolf or wolves over a carcass, but such incidents have been documented. Sometimes it's even worse. In 1991, a pack of eleven wolves attacked and killed two grizzly bear cubs on Denali's Sable Pass, in full view of several tour buses and bear technicians. The mother and surviving cub escaped, but were seriously injured. This incident (described in my book, *Out Among the Wolves*) caused researchers to re-evaluate some of their assumptions about the relationships between these two predators.

Your best opportunities to observe bears in the meat-eating mode are as follows: In Yellowstone's Hayden Valley there are numerous pull-outs. Early or late in the season this area of the park is a profitable place to spend some time. One turn-out overlooking the river even has a sign indicating it is a prime grizzly bear viewing area. Grizzlies here would be interacting with elk, bison, and mule deer. There are also other locations in the park, especially around Yellowstone Lake, where grizzlies can sometimes be seen fishing for native trout during the June spawning season. Another suggestion would be Alberta's Jasper National Park, especially along the Athabasca River. There are numerous pull-outs along the road here, and many afford commanding views of the river valley. Further north, in Denali National Park, there are several "hot-spots" along the 90 mile park road. The first is Sable Pass, about 40 miles from the George Parks Highway. There always seems to be some sort of daily excitement on Sable Pass. Polychrome Pass is another excellent viewing location, with the expansive Plains of Murie just below. The Toklat River, near the Toklat Ranger Station, is also worth visiting.

A number of videotapes sold commercially in the national and provincial park visitor centers contain footage of grizzlies attacking and killing large mammals. Those produced by Bob Landis of Billings, Montana are among the best known. It was Bob Landis who filmed the scene on Denali's Teklanika River in which the sow grizzly single-handedly brought down the bull caribou. Another option is to visit your local library or video store and rent or borrow the commercial or educational videotapes available there (such as the Audubon grizzly special or the 1966 *National Geographic* special featuring the work of the Craigheads in Yellowstone).

# 6

# RESTRAINED POWER

## *Grizzly Bear Behavior*

The grizzly was a paradox. Attacked in the wild by man it was a dangerous and deadly adversary, yet some individuals taken into captivity became docile and trustworthy. When in search of animal food to satisfy its hunger, the bear would strike down any large beast; and in the fighting ring it was a savage contender against a wild bull. But when grizzlies congregated with their kind to relish some desirable food—clover, acorsn, or whale—they ate together peaceably. If approached slowly and quietly by man, the bear would retire, unless it was a female with cubs. The grizzly had the power to be dominant, but only exercised it when alarmed, disturbed, or injured; otherwise it was a well-behaved member of the animal community.

—Tracy Storer and Lloyd Tevis, *California Grizzly*

GRIZZLIES, LIKE HUMANS, VARY CONSIDERABLY from individual to individual. While it is possible to broadly describe grizzly bear behavior in qualified terms, it is impossible to definitively predict grizzly bear behavior in every instance. Two sibling bears born an hour apart can react differently to the same event. They can also behave differently to the same event at different times. Even at different times on the same day. This is particularly important to remember when hiking and camping in grizzly country. You must assess every situation, every bear, on its own terms. Always remember that the bear in front of you could be a hothead with a fuse as short as that of Billy the Kid, or the resident matriarch with a temperament about as mellow as a bear ever had. And never forget that if you catch the lat-

Grizzlies begin to learn dominance roles as cubs, as can be seen in this aggressive display between two six month old cubs.

Bear society is matriarchal, with the mother teaching the cubs much of what they need to survive. Even in their third summer, these large cubs still nurse on their mother.

ter on a bad day (just pushed off a hard-won elk carcass by the resident bully) she could be as terrible as the former, and vice versa. So treat them all with respect and deference. The last is the most important concept to remember when interacting within any hierarchical organization, which is what bear society is. Always behave in deferential body language to a bear, never show any interest in cubs when around sows, and never make the potentially fatal mistake of establishing eye contact with any bear.

The range of grizzly behavior is apparent in these tales of two bears. For three summers in Denali National Park, I closely observed grizzly #102 (provided with a number because she was a problem bear and had to be fitted with a radio collar). She had three cubs with her in the first summer (1989), and two in the second and third. "Ragged Ear," as I called her (for more on this bear see "Ragged Ear of Sable Pass" in *A Republic of Rivers*), was the most insecure, nervous bear I ever observed. Ragged Ear was always looking around in a panic for other bears, panting, salivating, snapping her jaws at a mockingbird chattering in a tree over her head, jumping sideways at a butterfly, running off and abandoning her cubs at the sound (admittedly rare in the subarctic) of thunder. Her cubs, either because they were genetically coded or were environmentally imprinted, became behavioral clones of her. Eventually they, too, had to be radio-collared and put through aversive conditioning. I soon realized there was a social order among the bears of Sable Pass and, for whatever reason (certainly not size), she was the omega or bottom-ranking animal. All the other bears (and the adults were all female) routinely chased Ragged Ear from whatever food resources she was utilizing (berry patches or root beds). I was never certain what she was going to do, and always remained alert and at an extra safe distance while photographing her.

"Big Stoney," on the other hand, a grizzly closely watched for years by park naturalist Rick McIntyre on Highway Pass (and written about in his book, *Grizzly Cub*), was a self-confident and calm animal. If there was a disturbance on the tundra, she couldn't be bothered. Tourist buses with noisy diesel engines would gather around. Photographers would pile out of cars, extend tripods, and focus cameras the size of cannons. Rangers would actively superintend traffic. Big Stoney would yawn and stretch, blink a couple of times, and fall asleep right there on the side of the road. Year after year, she successfully raised litters to young adulthood. The last time I saw her, she was still the alpha female grizzly on the road corridor from the Toklat River to Thorofare Pass. To the uninformed eye, Big Stoney was just another sow grizzly. No different in appearance from Ragged Ear. But the two bears could not have been more different in terms of behavior. [Note: one of Big Stoney's cubs, "Little Stoney," later became something of an outlaw. Many familiar with the case believe his problem personality—breaking into cabins, approaching hikers and campers in the back-country, refusing to adapt to aversive conditioning—occurred not through any fault in upbringing but because at some point visitors illegally fed him, thus signing his death warrant].

Grizzly bear society is a matriarchal society. That much we do know. The males play no role in the upbringing of the young. In fact, they will sometimes attempt to kill the cubs when a meeting takes place. The cubs are taught everything they must know in order to survive by the mother. She teaches them, among other things, where the best plant foods are located, how to kill an elk or caribou, how to find the fish spawning streams, and when and in what manner to den. This educational process occurs over two, three, or more summers, but is generally concluded by the end of the third summer. At this point the mother breaks up the family, sometimes forcefully. The cub or cubs are then left to fend for themselves. It is at this stage that the young bears, or subadults, are most vulnerable to being killed by other bears, wolves or humans. Females often establish a residence adjoining or near that of their mothers'. Males tend to disperse more widely. As a result the male subadults experience greater mortality. I once observed a smallish four- or five-year-old bear chased by two wolves for half a mile on the Toklat bar. The last I saw, the wolves were still chasing the terrified bear upstream toward the glacier. This occcured about 1:30 in the morning (bear in mind there is no night at the 63rd parallel in the summer), and I was heading into camp after a 19-hour day, or I would have followed and attempted to discover the outcome of the situation. The incident underlines the precarious existence of grizzlies in the early years of adulthood, before they have achieved the large body mass and experience to consistently resolve dangerous situations in their favor.

Sometime after the fifth or sixth summer grizzly bears become sexually mature. The mating season occurs in the late spring and early summer. At this time males wander in search of receptive females, and females will also actively seek out mates. A story will illustrate. In mid-June of 1990 Eric Heyne, a colleague at the university, and I observed a male grizzly bear roaming the tundra on top of Sable Pass. His head was down and he appeared to be searching for some sort of a scent trail. He eventually disappeared over a ridge about a mile away. Twenty-four hours later, back on top of Sable Pass, Eric and I were approached by an adult female grizzly. She was full of energy and trotted directly to the car, cocking her head several times as a dog will when it wants to play. After spending two or three minutes curiously investigating the car (Eric and I inside), she suddenly lifted her head, smelling something. Moments later, on the tundra about fifty yards from the gravel pull-out, she found the scent trail of the male Eric and I had seen the previous day. It was uncanny. The female followed the scent trail exactly, following every twist and turn taken by the male. She eventually disappeared over the same ridge he had one day earlier.

It was on the same trip that Eric and I observed a large, dark-brown boar mating with a light-colored sow on the slopes of Cathedral Mountain (see photo on page xxx). This was the only time I observed this activity in Alaska. The strongest impression was of how large a boar grizzly was compared to an adult female. After a brief period of coupling, the female detached herself and led the boar around the side of the mountain into a more secluded area. She seemed completely docile in his presence, whereas she would normally avoid being within charging range of a boar. The most notable aspect of his

Even as adults grizzlies play. This bear is playing with a ball of its own shed fur.

This grizzly bear sow has just been stung on the muzzle by a honey bee. A mammalogist once assured me that animals do not feel pain as humans do. You be the judge.

behavior was that he was salivating profusely and seemed fascinated with her hindquarters. The breeding season is the only time of year that adult males and females will associate, unless they find a prodigious source of food, such as occurred at Yellowstone earlier in the century with the garbage dumps, and as still occurs at salmon and trout spawning streams. At that time grizzlies will become tolerant of one another and gather in groups of 40 or more to feed in relative peace. Most conflicts are settled through a show of force—posturing, raised hackles, growls, popping jaws, huffs, vague swipes, body slams—although violent battles sometimes insue for access to particularly good feeding locations.

As the Nobel laureate Konrad Lorenz discovered, aggression is ubiquitous in the animal world, from angelfish on a coral reef fighting over nesting locations to humans in jet planes fighting over desert oil. Grizzlies are no different. Aggression is one of the reasons the bears endured while many other Pleistocene megafauna are now extinct. Grizzlies evolved on the steppes of Eurasia. They encountered all sorts of dangerous animals (dire wolves, cave bears, saber-toothed tigers, human beings) on the wide-open grass plains and shrublands, and had to be aggressive or be destroyed. As a result they are behaviorally different than black bears, which evolved in the forests and had the ability to escape danger by climbing. Black bears as a rule are consequently less aggressive. Nevertheless, as the epigraph for this chapter indicates, grizzlies experience great individual variations. Some grizzlies, like the sow Marian studied by the John and Frank Craighead in Yellowstone, are less prone to violent incidents. Others are chronically involved in violent incidents. The same might be said for many mammals, including human beings.

Grizzlies also like to play. Some of my fondest memories are of watching bears at play. A few recollections:

A sow grizzly watches her cubs slide down a snowbank on Sable Pass. Finally she can stand it no longer. She climbs the snowbank and begins sliding down herself. On her back. On her side. On her stomach. Head first. Hindquarters first. For no other reason than because it is fun. Her cubs seem greatly amused by the

Two bears meet on a snowbank. Notice that the bear on the right has turned its head at an oblique angle to the other bear, and flattened its ears, thus signalling submission.

Grizzlies are intensely curious animals. They are always surveying their environment, sometimes rising on their hind legs for a better view.

sight of their normally solemn mother sliding down on top of her head with her rear paws sticking straight up in the air. So do about a hundred people in tourist buses parked along the road.

Two nearly grown cubs engage in a spirited but harmless boxing match on the top of Thorofare Pass. They stand upright on their hind legs and take swipes at each other. The boxing match then becomes a wrestling match. Then a half-mile race to a tundra pool. Then an extended bath in a tundra pool. Then a nap in the sun.

A four year old female grizzly on Stoney Hill lays on her back, with all four feet in the air, playing with a ball of her own shed fur. She kicks the ball up in the air, catches it, throws it to the side, picks it up, tosses it in the air. This goes on for five minutes.

Those who study animal behavior say that playfulness is a sign of intelligence. Such behaviors are found in otters, dolphins, and primates, animals known for their highly developed brains. Apparently, the grizzly has an intellect sufficiently large to permit it the luxury of idle recreation. Studies have shown that bears have the largest cranial capacity relative to body size of any predator group (felids, canids, ursids). Those tourists who saw the mother grizzly snowsliding with her cubs were given graphic evidence of that.

Toward the end of the summer, as the days shorten and the air temperatures cool, grizzlies become restless. They roam the country searching for whatever food they can find: nuts, berries, carcasses, small mammals. Each day the sense of urgency, of impending change, becomes greater. Bears live in a different world than a wolf or a mountain lion. The latter are active year-round and live pretty much from kill to kill. The grizzly bear sleeps during the winter. It has a knowledge of the future, and knows that soon the snows will come and that it must find a secure place to den. Just as important, the bear must absorb enough weight to live on its accumulated body fat until the next spring. The pregnant females are carrying the embryos fertilized earlier in the season. These embryos only begin to develop later in the season, after they are implanted on the uterine wall. This enables the young to be born in January or February, instead of at an inopportune earlier time. All bears begin to construct dens, probably by instinct, sometime in September or October, depending on local climatic conditions. For several days before entering the den, grizzlies become progressively sleepier. Finally, they can't stay awake. They crawl inside and collapse, while outside the snows fall and the winds blow.

Grizzlies in the wild can live into their twenties. A few live longer. Towards the end of life, bears, just like any mammal, slow down metabolically and become increasingly prone to disease and mishap. This is particularly evident when a large number of bears are gathered together near a large food source such as a salmon spawning stream. The older bears, though larger than many others, are often less active in the proceedings. They have arthritic pains from old wounds and broken bones. They may have worn teeth and find it painful to eat. Their senses may not be as sharp as they once were. Rangers who watch the resident bears each season are always saddened when an old favorite fails to appear one spring. Causes of mortality in wild populations are not well documented. Some bears, especially underweight bears, undoubtedly die in the den or shortly after awakening. This could particularly be the case following a drought year or a forest fire year when essential food sources are not available. Others succumb to parasites or other health problems. Still others are killed during the mating season, or while hunting dangerous animals such as bull moose, or by other predators, including wolves, grizzlies, and humans.

# 7

# BRIGHT SALMON, BIG BEARS

## *The Coastal Brown Bear of British Columbia and Alaska*

The low shale cliffs and meandering shoreline of Deadman Bay became Monarch's stronghold . . . Most of his early years had been spent on these raw, damp shores, and within a few miles of the sedge tide flat's around the Bay's perimeter he had learned some of his hardest lessons. He had feasted hugely on the crystal springs that roll into the Bay from the hills, for here were the rich salmon streams with their pea-sized gravel bars. In this district he had grown from a cub who list salmon catch to his elders to the mammoth he now was.
—Roger Caras, *Monarch of Deadman Bay: The Life and Death of a Kodiak Bear*

THE COASTAL BROWN BEAR (URSUS ARCTOS MID-dendorfi) inhabits the maritime regions of British Columbia and Alaska. This sub-species differs from the interior grizzly primarily in size. Brown bears routinely exceed 1,000 pounds, while interior grizzlies usually weigh considerably less than that. It is thought the brown bears attain greater size as a result of a more nutritious diet that includes searun salmon, scavenged sea mammals, and heavy berry crops. The largest population of brown bears in the world is found on Kodiak Island, about 150 miles southwest of Anchorage. Authorities believe there are around 3,000 bears on the island. Even in recent times, bears outnumbered human residents on the island. Each year, up to 130 different Kodiak bears gather on the O'Malley River, which lies between Karluk Lake and O'Malley Lake, to feed upon the spawning salmon. At this time, visitors observe the fascinating social aggregates and spontaneous hierarchies that are formed among the brown bears as they gather in dense populations to feed on the salmon. Normally retiring and intolerant of even their own species, brown bears at these times will risk confrontations in order to feast upon the abundant protein. Their appetites satiated, the huge brown bears are also more tolerant of humans and will even rest and sleep a few yards from unprotected viewing pads occupied by photographers.

There are several other locations in Alaska where this unique phenomena can be observed. Amazingly enough, no one has yet been killed at one of these sites. Probably the best known is MacNeil River State Game Sanctuary on the Alaska Peninsula, where visitors can observe up to sixty bears at one time feeding on salmon at McNeil River Falls. As with O'Malley, visitors must apply for permits through a state lottery system and are confined to several viewing platforms in the vicinity of the falls. Brooks Falls at Katmai National Park and Preserve on the Alaska Peninsula offers a situation similar to that at McNeil River. Reservations are necessary and Brooks Camp is becoming a more competitive and restrictive experience as visitor use increases. Stan Price State Wildlife Sanctuary at Pack Creek on Admiralty Island is similar to the others, as bears are observed fishing for sea-run salmon in Pack Creek and in the marshy intertidal areas. Fraser River on Kodiak Island is also becoming more popular. Like the rest, Fraser River can be reached only by floatplane or boat. For all these sites, the best time to visit is from early June through mid to late August during the peak salmon spawning season. If permits cannot be secured, a final possibility is to rent a plane from outfitters on the Kenai Peninsula. They routinely fly visitors over Cook Inlet for a view of brown bears feeding in remote salmon rivers and streams not yet developed by state or federal land management authorities. This can be quite expensive, and is better undertaken with a party of three or four. One danger here is that bears in more remote areas are not habituated to humans and will be less tolerant of visitors than those accustomed to human activity.

In Canada there are numerous opportunities to informally view bears along the coast of British Columbia. Virtually any outfitter who guides for salmon fishing can also guide visitors interested in observing brown bears. Midsummer would be the best time for this, when the bears are feeding on searun salmon. The best-known viewing area established to date is the Khutzeymateen River Sanctuary. The closest large city to the sanctuary is Ketchikan, Alaska. As with the other viewing areas to the north, Khutzeymateen offers photographers and other visitors the opportunity to observe brown bears fishing for salmon in the river and undertaking other activities in the intertidal areas.

To walk in any of these areas is an experience to remember. The dimensions of the tracks are stunning, even if you are accustomed to tracking large bears. The sheer number of bears is overwhelming, and leaves one both happy and sad. Happy that so many endure. Sad that we will never see such bear congregations again near the mouth of the Columbia River, or on the shores of Drake's Bay at Point Reyes just north of San Francisco.

# 8

# THE RELUCTANT HOST AND THE UNINVITED GUEST

## *Bears and People*

Enter Glacier National Park and you entered the homeland of the grizzly bear. We are uninvited guests here, intruders, the bear our reluctant host.

—Edward Abbey, "Fire Lookout: Numa Ridge"
*Abbey's Road*

About once a year I visit my parent's home in Denver. Usually this is around the Christmas holidays. For the time I am a guest in their home, I must obey their rules. My rowdy friends from college days must behave themselves. Especially Roger. No wrestling matches after dinner with my brothers in the living room. No rock tapes on the sound system. Quiet hours from eight at night until six in the morning. No raiding the refrigerator in the middle of the night as this will awaken my father. And so on. The same principles of courtesy and respect apply when I enter the wilderness domain of the grizzly. I must change my behavior. This is not my home, after all. It is, however, the year-round residence of the bears. I am only a visitor. I cannot, therefore, eat in my tent, much as I would like to. Nor

When camping in grizzly country, it is advisable to place the tent near a substantial tree that can be climbed if necessary. Pictured here is the author's 1992 fall hunting camp above the Sheenjek River in the Arctic National Wildlife Refuge.

can I store food near where I camp. If I'm hungry in the middle of the night I must listen to my stomach growl. I cannot hike on the trails after dark. I must scrupulously maintain and clean my campsite. I do all this, and more, as much to protect the lives of bears as I do my own. A bear that has tasted human food—even something as seemingly innocuous as half a candy bar—is a bear possibly marked for death in a "control action." Two years after a visit to Yellowstone, you might pick up a newspaper and read that park rangers killed a sow grizzly and her two cubs following an incident at a backcountry campsite. If you were the person who left the treat that got this bear originally hooked on refined sugar, you bear a moral responsibility for these deaths, or worse, for the mutilation or death of a person she later attacks. So when the national park or provincial park rangers orient you to the backcountry rules, please listen carefully to their admonishments and scrupulously adhere to their recommendations.

One of the most important things to remember when

hiking in grizzly country is that you must not surprise the bears. When confronted unexpectedly at close range, grizzlies will often charge. They do this more out of fear than out of petulance. You are suddenly there—thirty or twenty or ten yards away—and they are not sure what you are or what you're intentions are. So they charge, and sometimes that charge culminates in a mauling or lethal attack. The way to decrease the chances of a catastrophic encounter in the backcountry is to make noise that will identify you as human while you are hiking. There are a number of ways to achieve this. Some people carry bells on their persons or on their packs. Others vocalize loudly. I sing loudly and occassionally clap my hands. I've been known to sing all the songs to the Beatle's *Rubber Soul* album during an afternoon hike. Sometimes, if there's fresh scat and tracks on the trail, I periodically cut loose with a rebel yell. If the brush is thick, I move much more slowly than I would in open country. I do this to give any bears ahead an opportunity to clear out of the country. If the bears know you are coming they will normally—unless they are somewhat touched in the head or extremely hungry—yield the trail. A final piece of advice: try to travel in a group if you can, as bears are less likely to attack a group of people than one or two persons.

If you have taken these precautions, but are still confronted with a charging bear, you have several options. Running is not one of them, unless you have a tree a few steps away and can instantly reach it. Remember that mature grizzlies can jump and reach ten or twelve feet into a tree, and if sufficiently motivated by fear, anger, hunger, or crankiness can probably scramble into the lower branches and attain greater heights. Bear managers in the Alaskan national parks now recommend that if charged, you wave your hands and make a considerable amount of noise, so that the bear can properly assess what you are and what your possible intentions are. If the bear realizes the intruder is human, and not another grizzly or a wolf, it may break off the charge. Even if you take all of these steps, you may still find yourself about to be attacked. Once the bear is on you, most experts recommend that you assume a "cannonball" or fetal po-

On August 4, 1961 Napier Shelton, a graduate student from Duke University, was core-boring spruce trees in then-Mckinley National Park. A sow with two cubs suddenly appeared. Shelton climbed this tree, the one on which he had been boring, to escape. The sow worked her way up through the branches, biting both his legs as he kicked and climbed higher. He waited in the tree one half hour before climbing down and seeking assistance. Photograph by Adolph Murie. Courtesy of the University of Alaska.

sition, protecting your abdomen and chest with your legs and the back of your neck with your hands. Do not move and try not to make any sounds, even if you are being mauled. The idea is to convince the bear you are not a threat. After the initial attack is over, and the bear has departed the vicinity, do not immediately shout or try to seek assistance. There is a possibility the bear is still in the area, and will return to continue the attack if it perceives you are not "dead."

GRIZZLY BEARS

It is important not to resist a grizzly attack unless you are armed with a weapon sufficiently powerful to kill the bear. Such weapons—12-gauge shotguns with rifled slugs or buckshot; high-powered rifles; .44 magnum revolvers—are prohibited in the national and provincial parks, and are discouraged on other public lands as they often pose more of a threat to people, through accidents, than to bears. Nevertheless, such weapons have saved lives. In 1992 a Soldotna, Alaska hiker survived a grizzly attack only because he carried a .44 magnum revolver on his belt and was able to shoot the bear to death as it mauled him. He required extensive reconstructive surgery on his head and face, but he did live. In other cases, armed hikers have, through accidents, been permanently crippled or killed by their own firearms. Some authorities, as with Stephen Herrero in his seminal book *Bear Attacks*, recommend carrying firearms in some situations. Others, like biologist Charles Jonkel, suggest carrying one of the aerosol pepper sprays. In Alaska I carry either a high-powered rifle or a magnum revolver while hiking outside parklands, especially while salmon fishing or picking blueberries in brushy areas. Having seen grizzlies up close for many years inside Denali, and observed their mercurial nature and their impressive muscular power, I have nothing but respect for their ability to inflict massive destruction upon human beings. As a former Marine rifleman, my knowledge of firearm safety and use goes back several decades; I would not recommend these dangerous weapons for those not willing to spend the time to learn and master them.

While on the trail or hiking off the trail (not a recommended activity), always avoid the following: kill sites of any origin or ownership (whether occupied by foxes, coyotes, wolverines, wolves or grizzlies); grizzly bear dens; grizzly bear daybeds; areas of high-density bear use (spawning salmon or trout streams); areas of low visibility and concentrated bear activity (valley trails through dense vegetation when open highland trails are available). As was mentioned earlier, never hike at night in grizzly country. In many parts of North America, grizzly bears have become largely nocturnal to avoid contact with humans. Similarly, try not to hike during the early

Grizzly encounters occur periodically on the backroads of Alaska and northwestern Canada. The bad thing about roads in grizzly country is that they increase the opportunities for poachers. Bear gall-bladders are worth many thousands of dollars in Asia.

Periodically, backcountry areas in the parks and forests must be closed because of grizzly bear activity. These units are closed for a variety of reasons: a recent human/bear incident, a fresh kill site, or feeding bears near the trail. Always heed these posted warnings.

Barren-Ground Caribou. Bull caribou are hunted by wolves and grizzlies in the fall after the rut, when the bulls are in a weakened state.

Moose are found throughout the range of the North American grizzly. They are most vulnerable to predation in the autumn, following the rut. Moose calves are hunted in the spring.

When grizzlies are stressed they pant, drool, pop their jaws, vocalize, or direct their nervousness to an alternative object, in this case an alpine willow branch. Here the bear has become stressed by a park tour bus with a loud diesel engine.

Grizzly bears are attracted to unusual objects in their territory, such as road signs, which they bite, claw, and rub against. This sign on top of Sable Pass in Denali National Park has to be regularly replaced, so extensive are the bear markings. Most behavioralists believe the grizzly is not a territorial species.

Coastal Brown Bear. Kenai National Wildlife Refuge, Alaska. These are the largest bears in the world, with mature animals weighing in excess of 1,500 pounds and standing over ten feet tall when erect.

Devil's Club is common in brown bear habitat. The bears eat the tender shoots in the spring, and the clumped red berries in late summer and autumn. Devil's Club, covered with sharp thorns, is the nemesis of the backcountry hiker in brown bear country.

Whether these grizzlies have a future will depend on whether we can save habitat.

An anestheticized and radio-collared grizzly bear. This animal will give researchers valuable data about grizzly habitat use.

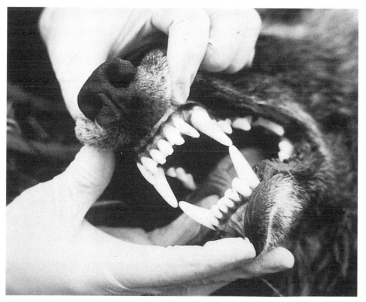

The pristine condition of the teeth indicates this is a subadult grizzly bear. Courtesy of U.S.F.W.S.

morning and evening hours. If you see a bear on the trail or in the vicinity, you may have to postpone or completely change your travel plans. Never approach a bear in the wild. If you are photographing away from your vehicle, stay one-quarter mile away from the bears. Remember that the land belongs to the bears. I have more than once had to hike out of a drainage and find an alternative route back to camp because there were grizzlies ahead on the trail. Sometimes this is quite inconvenient—late in the day, a cold rain, heavy winds, blistered feet—but it is better than having reconstructive surgery.

Once in your backcountry camp, you must exercise several precautions. The first is to separate your cooking and food storage area from your sleeping area. The distance between the two areas should be at least a couple of hundred yards. All food should be stored in the bear-proof food containers that are now almost universally provided by the national and provincial parks. These containers should be suspended from a rope high in trees where they cannot be reached by bears. If you have been fishing or hunting, keep all game meat in the food preparation area. Keep your sleeping area immaculate. Wash up every day and do not sleep in the same clothes in which you gutted out fish or game. Avoid using colognes, deodorants, or any other artificial scents. Try to smell like a human being, again so that the bear can properly identify you. Some experts recommend that you avoid sexual activity in camp, as this may attract bears, and that women having their periods avoid the backcountry at that time. Apparently there have been attacks that have been possibly linked to both.

In six years of observing grizzlies in Alaska, often at close range, I had only a handful of encounters that still make me feel uncomfortable to think about. In one instance, nature writer Rick Bass and I were hiking near the headwaters of Igloo Creek. The uplands there are treeless tundra. Rick was walking about ten feet ahead of me. I had just finished pointing out to Rick where I had first seen a grizzly bear in August, 1988 when, incredible but true, an adult grizzly jumped down from a rock outcropping 27 feet in front of Rick (we later paced it off). We immediately stopped and instinctively crouched

A tripod used by researchers to weigh a grizzly.

down. I recognized from the radio collar, hair color and body shape that this bear was "Frisky," a three-hundred-pound, five-year-old male and one of the problem griz-zlies in the Sable Pass area. The bear seemed surprised and confused to see us in his path and stood rigidly still. Rick was in an extremely exposed and dangerous posi-tion, being so close to the bear. I whispered to Rick to freeze and to not look the bear in the eye. The bear was standing broadside to us and did not move. He flexed the

Grizzly bear viewing spot in Hayden Valley, Yellowstone National Park. From this location park visitors can safely observe grizzlies in the wild. Such officially designated sites are also found in Alaska and the provincial parks of Canada.

In this experiment on the Pine Butte Grizzly Preserve in Montana, an electrically wired fence has been constructed around a dead horse. Should the hot fence deter grizzlies, all cook tents in the Bob Marshall Wilderness Area may soon be outfitted with mobile electrical units, thus reducing a chronic conflict between humans and grizzlies.

muscles in his body, which caused his hair to stand erect. This gave him a more massive appearance, and is a normal aggressive display when bears are alarmed. A few tense seconds later, Frisky vocalized with a low growl, turned and walked away, looking back once to watch us. We remained perfectly still, our heads at oblique angles to the bear. Denali has never had a fatal bear attack, but it came close that afternoon. If the timing of our chance encounter had been slightly different, we could have been so close to the bear that an attack would have been unavoidable. Similarly, if our reaction had been different the outcome might have changed. Both of us may have been mauled and possibly worse.

Another case occurred after I hiked five miles up the Savage River in order to find a pair of interlocked moose antlers that Japanese photographer, Michio Hoshino, and Denali ranger Rick McIntyre had told me about. The bulls had died while battling during the rut, their antlers forever joined. Rick and Michio said the antlers made a stunning photograph, with the terminal glaciers of the Savage River in the background. I hiked five miles up the Savage, at least by the topographic map, but never found the antlers. It was a tough hike, too. There are no maintained trails into the valley. In some places I had to wade up the middle of the river (this was late summer and the water was low) because of the extensive riparian brush. On the return trip I pulled some cartilege in my right knee. Bushwacking through the dense alpine willows soon became an ordeal. The knee eventually stiffened to the extent that I used my camera tripod as a crutch. Toward the end of the ten-mile jaunt, I began to make expressions of discomfort. There was no one around, so at times I vocalized quite freely. When I reached the confluence of Jenny Creek and the Savage River, I sat down to take off my boots so that I could wade across the creek. This site is about half a mile below the Savage River Campground, where I was camped. As I sat there a middle-aged couple ran down the opposing hill, waving their hands and shouting. The man looked somewhat like the new dean for the College of Arts so, to be on the safe side, I waved back. I then stood up with my boots around my neck, took my tripod in hand, and waded

Grizzly bears feeding on grass in the high mountains, mid-summer. These bears are approximately 200 yards away. They are aware of the observer. If you encounter a situation like this, do not attempt to close the distance. Alter your travel plans so as not to conflict with bear activities or routes of travel.

across Jenny Creek. When I reached the top of the cut-bank, the out-of-breath couple told me that a grizzly bear had closely followed me for the last several hundred yards, stopping when I stopped, and had been standing right behind me, perhaps ten feet away, as I took off my boots. I was a little skeptical about this, but then a second, younger couple ran over from another vantage point to confirm the report. They had watched the whole thing with binoculars and couldn't believe I hadn't known about the bear. The bear had run away when the middle-aged couple started shouting. I recrossed the stream and retraced my steps and, sure enough, there were fresh grizzly tracks imprinted in the sand over my own tracks. In retrospect, the lesson is clear: don't hobble around and sound injured in grizzly country.

Even if you scrupulously adhere to the park or forest regulations, situations like these can still arise in which you may find yourself in an undesirable situation. Grizzly country will always be a dangerous place, and we assume certain risks when we journey there. I think, though, it was the venerated wildlife biologist, Aldo Leopold, who expressed it best when he wrote in an essay on grizzlies, that "It must be poor life that achieves freedom from fear." Grizzlies and people can coexist, but we must show the kind of respect our forefathers did, and the native Americans did before them. The bears are, as the nature writer Edward Abbey said, our reluctant hosts. They roamed the mountains of the New World when our ancestors worshipped cave bear skulls. With a bit of deference on our part, they will still inhabit these mountains when posterity is exploring the stars of Ursa Major.

# 9

# LAST STAND
## *Grizzly Bears and the Future*

The grizzly needs protection at once, needs your active interest now. He is making his last stand and is surrounded by relentless foes. Protection only will save him and enable him to perpetuate himself. Without the grizzly the wilds would be dull, the canyon and the crag would lose their eloquent appeal. This wild uncrowned king has won his place in nature which no other animal can fill. We need the grizzly bear—the King of the Wilderness World . . . the grizzly populations [in Oregon and California] might be more quickly affected by restocking. A few grizzlies could be trapped in Yellowstone and set free in these other National Parks. The problem of restocking unoccupied areas would not be difficult . . . He is the greatest animal that is without a voice . . . He is the most impressive animal on the continent.

—Enos Mills, The Grizzly (1919)

I RECENTLY JOURNEYED OVERLAND FROM MY home of six years in Alaska to Colorado. This leisurely trip of nearly four thousand miles crossed the heart of North American grizzly habitat. Along the way I stopped and explored the major parks and preserves supporting grizzlies: Wrangell/St. Elias (Alaska), Kluane (Yukon Territory), Nahanni (Northwest Territory), Muncho Lake and Stone Mountain (British Columbia), Willmore Wilderness-Jasper-Banff (Alberta), Waterton-Glacier (Alberta) Glacier (Montana), Pine Butte Grizzly Preserve (Montana), and Yellowstone-Grand Teton (Wyoming). Grizzly habitat remained surprisingly consistent through this extensive region, which ranged from boreal forests in the high latitudes to old growth conifer forests in the more temperate latitudes. The plant associations changed grad-

If one more person jumps on the left side of the bus, it just may
tip over. The extended cameras from the windows gives a sense
of how popular the bear is. Over 90% of all visitors to Denali
see a grizzly in the wild, and most visitors report on question-
naires that what they most wanted to see was a grizzly.

ually, with the white spruce of the northern light country
soon replaced by the Englemann spruce so characteristic
of the Rockies, and the ubiquitous paper birch of the
Great North Woods supplanted by the quaking aspen.
Visually there was little difference. The landforms—high
glaciated peaks, clear streams, rocky canyons, wide river
valleys—displayed remarkable continuity.

From north to south I noticed progressive develop-
mental pressure on bear habitat. Alaska, of course, remained almost wholly pristine. Concern for any local
situations is mitigated by the fact that there are 30,000
grizzlies in the state and that the severe subpolar climate
will forever preclude livestock grazing and large human
populations. Similarly, in the Yukon I would drive all
day and pass one quiet village of eighty or ninety souls.
Travel in this sparsely populated province, as in neigh-
boring Alaska, was best accomplished by float plane or
Piper Supercub. There were a few hard-rock mines in the
Yukon, and a scattering of timber companies, but re-
source projects were restricted by the short work season,

the shortage of electrical power, and the isolation from open water seaports and railheads (Ft. Nelson, B.C. is the closest railhead to the Yukon). By the time I reached Alberta and the Rockies proper, the grizzly habitat situation had begun to change. There were bustling towns every twenty or thirty miles, even in remote mountains. Oil and gas facilities appeared at regular intervals, as did evidence of extensive timber operations. Both activities took people and machinery into once-isolated wilderness habitat. Livestock grazing, as elsewhere in the West, was pursued on the scale of an industry. Recreational development—ski resorts and second home subdivisions—filled valleys and associated side-valleys, in most cases conflicting with bear habitat.

Whereas Kluane Provincial Park in the Yukon was not commercially developed in any meaningful way, Banff Provincial Park in Alberta had four-lane highways, clover-leaf interchanges and an internationally-known resort system. Across the border in the United States, Glacier and Yellowstone National Parks were also heavily utilized and managed. Unlike Canada, where the sheer size of the provincial wildlands has offered the grizzly some protection from development, the bear in the Lower 48 has found itself in a precarious situation. The enormous volumes of habitat are simply not there. They all disappeared earlier in the century. At this writing, the grizzly in the coterminus 48 states is being managed as a threatened species under the Endangered Species Act. The largest population exists around Glacier National Park and the Bob Marshall Wilderness Area, with an estimated 440 to 680 bears. Greater Yellowstone protects perhaps at least 250 grizzlies. The other four ecosystems—Cabinet-Yaak in northwestern Montana, Selkirk in northern Idaho, Selway-Bitterroot in eastern Idaho, and Northern Cascades in Washington—have extremely small, low density populations.

Although the Yellowstone and Glacier ecosystems will probably always have grizzlies, it is not certain these other four populations can sustain themselves in perpetuity. Clearly, this will not happen unless the four ecosystems are carefully attended to by state and federal authorities. Conceivably this will include the augmentation of endangered populations with new, translocated members. Given the propensity of bears to return to their home ranges, restocking could be a difficult process. One source of hope is interspecific crossfostering. In this technique, grizzly cubs are placed into the natal den of a female black bear. The grizzlies are then raised in a different educational environment. Black bears are a more retiring, forest-dwelling bear and generally have fewer conflicts with humans than grizzlies. Interspecific crossfostering represents a gentler way of reintroducing grizzlies into areas in which their numbers may be dwindling or abscent.

A final grizzly ecosystem that has received increasing attention in the 1990s is found in the San Juan Mountains of southwestern Colorado. The state recorded its last known grizzly on September 23, 1979, when a 16-year-old female was killed by a hunter in the South San Juan Wilderness Area. The region in which the bear lived is just north of the New Mexico border. A two-year effort was undertaken to determine the status of the species in the area. The results were inconclusive. Scientists found dig sites for various rooted plants, a dig site for a marmot, and a partially collapsed den. There was also a sighting of a sow and two cubs. At that site researchers found a large dig site and a quantity of blond hair. Microscopic analysis of the hair was undertaken, with negative results. This subject was covered in detail in my 1987 book, *Wildlife in Peril: The Endangered Mammals of Colorado.* Since that time, there have been unconfirmed sightings and reports of grizzly activity in the ecosystem. More recently, a number of prominent nature writers, including David Petersen, Doug Peacock, Rick Bass, and Peter Matthiessen have visited the area and written articles and/or books about the population. Bear scats and hair samples have been found and turned in to authorities for analysis, but so far no definitive results have been achieved. The revised U.S. Fish and Wildlife Service recovery plan for grizzly bears (1991) lists the Colorado population as one to be monitored and evaluated on an ongoing basis. If a bear or bears is/are confirmed, a number of decisions will have to be made, under the Endangered Species Act, as to protection and

East Fork of Navajo River headwaters, South San Juan Wilderness, Colorado. On September 24, 1979 a grizzly bear was killed in the sidehill park near the center of the photograph. Some believe this was the last Southwestern grizzly; others maintain additional grizzlies inhabit this remote area.

augmentation of the isolated population. Those interested in the most up-to-date analysis of the subject should read David Petersen's *Ghost Grizzlies* (Henry Holt, 1995).

What all the threatened populations have in common is a habitat problem. The first step in preserving habitat is to change attitudes through education. That is what this book has been about. Probably the most important thing readers can do in this respect is to introduce their children to bears and bear country. In my case, that educational process began at an early age when my mother read Ernest Thompson Seton's *Wahb* to my brothers and me. Later, my father took us on a long road trip to hike in grizzly country. Even children of seven or eight can hike several miles a day in the high mountains. I took my son for his first walk in Alaskan grizzly country when was he was two weeks old. Admitedly he was in a back carrier, and pretty much oblivious to the import of the experience, but at least it got him started, and planted the image of wildness somewhere in his consciousness (as well as a deep memory of mosquitoes). The second step is to participate, if only through membership, in the various organizations, such as Defenders of Wildlife, the Wilderness Society, the Audubon Society, and the Sierra Club, that are fighting for the grizzly and grizzly habitat. The third and final step is especially important in a democracy, and that is to vote your values. All of us working together and remaining vigilant can hopefully pass on these wonderful lands, these wild bears, to our children as they were handed down to us.

How prophetic Enos Mills, the founder of Rocky Mountain National Park, was in writing of the grizzly nearly eight decades ago. How far ahead of his time, both in recognizing that the bear would be saved only by decisive action and in forseeing the need to restock grizzlies in areas formerly inhabited. At the time he wrote those words, the grizzly still lived in Mexico, the American Southwest, and the Pacific Coast states. Today it is probably forever gone from the Sierra Madres of Mexico, although it may one day recolonize the Pacific Coast states, and be restocked in Colorado. In those areas where the grizzly persists, it does so only through our generosity. Frank Craighead spoke for many when he wrote in his 1979 book, *Track of the Grizzly*:

Alive, the grizzly is a symbol of freedom and understanding—a sign that man can learn to conserve what is left of the earth. Extinct, it will be another fading testimony to things man should have learned more about but was too preoccupied with himself to notice. In its beleagured condition, it is above all a symbol of what man is doing to the entire planet. If we can learn from these experiences, and learn rationally, both the grizzly and man may have a chance to survive.

# *Appendix 1*

## Further Reading on Grizzly Bears

Brown, David E. *The Grizzly in the Southwest: Documentary of an Extinction.* Tucson: University of Arizona Press, 1985.

Caras, Roger. *Monarch of Deadman Bay.* Lincoln: University of Nebraska Press, 1990.

Chapman, J. A. and G. A. Feldhammer. *Wild Mammals of North America.* Baltimore: The Johns Hopkins University Press, 1982.

Craighead, Frank. *Track of the Grizzly.* San Francisco: Sierra Club Books, 1979.

Craighhead, John J.; J.S. Sumner; and G. B. Scaggs, *A Definitive System for Analysis of Grizzly Bear Habitat and Other Wilderness Resources* (Western-Wildlife Institute Monograph No. 1). Missoula, Montana: University of Montana Foundation, 1982.

Erickson, A. W. *Evaluation of the Suitability of the Gila Wilderness for Re-establishment of the Grizzly Bear.* Report to the U.S. Forest Service, Southwestern Regional Office, Contract 6-369-74. Typescript. (for portions of this see Murray, John A. *The Gila Wilderness.* Albuquerque: University of New Mexico Press, 1988).

Herrero, Stephen. *Bear Attacks: Their Causes and Avoidance.* New York: Nick Lyons Books, 1985.

McNamee, Thomas. *The Grizzly Bear.* New York: McGraw Hill, 1985.

Mills, Enos. *The Grizzly Bear.* Sausalito, CA: Comstock Editions, Inc., 1973.

Murie, Adolph. *A Naturalist in Alaska.* Tucson: University of Arizona Press, 1990.

Murie, Adolph. *The Grizzlies of Mount McKinley.* Seattle: University of Washington Press, 1982.

Murray, John A. "A Last Look at the Grizzly: The Story of a Two Year Search for Grizzly Bears in Colorado." *Colorado Outdoors* 34 (6): 28–33, 1985.

Murray, John A. *Wildlife in Peril: The Endangered Mammals of Colorado.* Boulder, Colorado: Roberts Rinehart, 1987.

Murray, John A., and David E. Brown. *The Last Grizzly, and Other Southwestern Bear Stories.* Tucson: University of Arizona Press, 1989.

Murray, John A. *The Great Bear: Contemporary Writings on the Grizzly.* Seattle: Alaska Northwest, 1991.

Murray, John A., Sherry Pettigrew, and Monte Hummel. *Wild Hunters: Predators in Peril.* Boulder, Colorado: Roberts Rinehart, 1992.

Peacock, Doug. *Grizzly Years.* New York: Henry Holt, 1990.

Petersen, David. *Ghost Grizzlies.* New York: Henry Holt, 1995.

Roosevelt, Theodore. Paul Schullery, ed. *American Bears.* Boulder: Colorado Associated University Press, 1983.

Schullery, Paul. *The Bears of Yellowstone.* Boulder: Roberts Rinehart, 1986.

Schullery, Paul. "Yellowstone Grizzlies: The New Breed." *National Parks* (Nov/Dec 1989): 25–29.

Seton, Ernest Thompson. T*he Biography of a Grizzly.* Lincoln: University of Nebraska Press, 1985.

Shepard, Paul, and Barry, Sanders. *The Sacred Paw: The Bear in Nature, Myth and Literature.* New York: Viking Penguin, Inc., 1985.

Storer, Tracy I. and Lloyd, Tevis. *California Grizzly.* Lincoln: University of Nebraska Press, 1985.

Wright, William. *The Grizzly Bear.* Lincoln: University of Nebraska Press, 1987.

# Appendix 2

**Where to see Grizzly Bears and Brown Bears in Alaska, Canada, and the Continental United States**

A. Alaska

Dalton Highway (Contact: Bureau of Land Management, 1150 University Avenue, Fairbanks, Alaska 99709)

Denali National Park (Contact: Superintendent, Denali National Park and Preserve, Denali Park, Alaska 99755)

Arctic National Wildlife Refuge (Contact: Refuge Manager, Arctic National Wildlife Refuge, Fairbanks, Alaska 99702)

Gates of the Arctic National Park (Contact: Superintendent, Gates of the Arctic National Park, Fairbanks, Alaska 99702)

McNeil River State Game Sanctuary (Contact: Alaska Department of Fish and Game, 333 Raspberry Road, Anchorage, Alaska 99518)

Anan Creek (Contact: U.S. Forest Service Wrangell Ranger District, PO Box 51, Wrangell, Alaska 99929)

Pack Creek (Contact: Admiralty Island National Monument, 8461 Old Dairy Road, Juneau, Alaska 99801)

O'Malley River (Contact: Kodiak National Wildlife Refuge, 1390 Buskin River Road, Kodiak, Alaska 99615)

Brooks River Camp (Contact: Superintendent, Katmai National Park and Preserve, PO BOX 7, King Salmon, Alaska 99613)

Stan Price State Wildlife Sanctuary (Contact: Alaska Dept. of Fish and Game, Division of Wildlife Conservation, Area Biologist, 304 Lake Street - Room 103, Sitka, Alaska 99835)

Fraser River (Contact: Kodiak National Wildlife Refuge, 1390 Bushkin River Road, Kodiak, Alaska 99615)

Alaska Peninsula/Cook Inlet (Contact: Chamber of Commerce - Homer, Kenai Ninilchik, or Soldotna, Alaska; ask for air taxi operators and outfitters who provide tours or transport to this area)

B. Canada

Yukon

Kluane Provincial Park (Contact: Director General, Parks Canada, Department of Indian and Northern Affairs, 400 Laurier Avenue West, Ottawa, Ontario K1A 0H4)

Northwest Territories

Nahanni Provincial Park (Contact: Director General, Parks Canada, Department of Indian and Northern Affairs, 400 Laurier Avenue West, Ottawa, Ontario K1A 0H4)

British Columbia

Mount Robson Provincial Park (Contact: Director, Parks Branch, Department of Recreation and Conservation, Parliament Buildings, Victoria, British Columbia; or Regional Supervisor, Mount Robson Provincial Park, Red Pass, British Columbia)

Muncho Lake Provincial Park (Contact: Director, Parks Branch, Department of Recreation and Conservation, Parliament Buildings, Victoria, British Columbia)

Stone Mountain Provincial Park (Contact: Director, Parks Branch, Department of Recreation and Conservation, Parliament Buildings, Victoria, British Columbia)

Bowron Lake Provincial Park (Contact: Director, Parks Branch, Department of Recreation and Conservation, Parliament Buildings, Victoria, British Columbia; or Regional Supervisor, Bowron Lake Provincial Park, Box 33, Barkerville, British Columbia)

Khutzeymateen River Sanctuary (Contact: Khutzeymateen River Sanctuary, New Denver, British Columbia VOG 1S0)

Wells Gray Provincial Park (Contact: Director, Parks Branch, Department of Recreation and Conservation, Parliament Buildings, Victoria, British Columbia; or Regional Supervisor, Wells Gray Provincial Park, Box 297, Clearwater, British Columbia)

Kokanee Glacier Provincial Park (Contact: Director, Parks Branch, Department of Recreation and Conservation, Parliament Buildings, Victoria, British Columbia; or Regional Supervisor, Kokanee Glacier Provincial Park, RR 3, Nelson, British Columbia)

Alberta

Jasper Provincial Park (Contact: Superintendent, Jasper Provincial Park, Jasper, Alberta TOE 1EO)

Banff National Park (Contact: Superintendent, Banff Provincial Park, Banff, Alberta)

Waterton Lakes Provincial Park (Contact: Superintendent, Waterton Lakes Provincial Park, Waterton Lakes, Alberta, TOK 2MO)

C. Coterminous United States

Montana

Glacier National Park (Contact: Superintendent, Glacier National Park, West Glacier, Montana 59936)

Pine Butte Grizzly Preserve (Contact: Preserve Manager, Pine Butte Preserve and Guest Ranch, HC 58, Choteau, Montana 59422)

Bob Marshall Wilderness Area (Contact: Supervisor, Lewis and Clark National Forest, Federal Building, Great Falls, Montana 59401; and Supervisor, Flathead National Forest, 290 North Main, Kalispell, Montana 59901)

Wyoming

Yellowstone National Park (Contact: Superintendent, Yellowstone National Park, Wyoming 82190)

Idaho

Grizzlies are present in small, low-density populations in the Selway-Bitterroot Wilderness and in the Selkirk Mountains. These are not recommended viewing areas, although at some point in the distant future the populations could grow to the extent that they might become reliable viewing areas.

Washington

As with the two Idaho populations, grizzlies are present in small, low-density numbers in North Cascades National Park. At the present time this is not a recommended area for grizzly bear viewing. (Contact: Superintendent, North Cascades National Park, Sedro Woolley, Washington 98284)

Colorado

The last grizzly was killed near Blue Lake, in the South San Juan Wilderness Area, on September 23, 1979. No confirmed sightings have been made since then.

# *Appendix 3*

## Grizzlies in Zoological Parks

Grizzlies and/or Brown Bears can be viewed in the following zoos:

Anchorage, Alaska; Birmingham, Alabama; Montgomery, Alabama; Chaffee, California; Sacramento, California; San Diego, California; San Francisco, California; Colorado Springs, Colorado; Denver, Colorado; Washington, D.C.; Atlanta, Georgia; Pocatello, Idaho; Chicago, Illinois; Indianapolis, Indiana; Manhattan, Kansas; Baton Rouge, Louisiana; Baltimore, Maryland; Detroit, Michigan; Duluth, Minnesota; St. Paul, Minnesota; Jackson, Mississippi; St. Louis, Missouri; Omaha, Nebraska; Buffalo, Syracuse, New York City, Utica, New York; Bismark, North Dakota; Minot, North Dakota; Cleveland, Ohio; Columbus, Ohio; Oklahoma City, Oklahoma; Tulsa, Oklahoma; Portland, Oregon; Erie, Pennsylvania; Pittsburgh, Pennsylvania; Sioux Falls, South Dakota; Memphis, Tennessee; El Paso, Houston, San Antonio, Texas; Salt Lake City, Utah; Seattle, Washington; Madison, Milwaukee, Racine Wisconsin.

# Appendix 4

## Organizations Involved in Preserving Grizzly Bears

Canadian Wildlife Federation
2740 Queensview Drive, Ottawa, Ontario, Canada K2B 1A2

Commission on National Parks and Protected Areas (subgroup of IUCN), IUCN Headquarters, CH1196 Gland, Switzerland

Defenders of Wildlife
1244 19th Street, NW, Washington, DC 20036

Great Bear Foundation
PO Box 2699, Missoula, Montana 59806

Greater Yellowstone Coalition
PO Box 1874, 13 South Willson, Bozeman, MT 59771

International Association for Bear Research and Management, Department of Forestry, Wildlife and Fisheries, University of Tennessee, Knoxville, TN 37901

IUCN (International Union for the Conservation of Nature and Natural Resources, World Conservation Union, Avenue du Mont-Blanc CH-1196 Gland, Switzerland

National Audubon Society
950 Third Avenue, New York, NY 10022

National Wildlife Federation
1400-Sixteenth Street, NW, Washington, DC 20036

The Nature Conservancy
1815 North Lynn Street, Arlington, VA 22209

North American Bear Society
PO Box 9281
Scottsdale, AZ 85252

Sierra Club
730 Polk Street
San Francisco, CA 94109

The Wilderness Society
900 17th Street, NW Washington, DC 2006-2596

Wildlife Conservation International
New York Zoological Society,
185th Street and South Boulevard, Building A
Bronx, New York 10460

World Wildlife Fund
1250 24th St. N.W.,
Washington, D.C. 20037

# *Index*

INDEX